Ruel O. Redinger is a commercially successful silversmith and a widely acknowledged expert in the field.

RUEL O. REDINGER

SILVER

An Instructional Guide to the Silversmith's Art

739.2
Rod

A SPECTRUM BOOK   Prentice-Hall, Inc., Englewood Cliffs, N.J. 07632

Library of Congress Cataloging in Publication Data

Redinger, Ruel O.
     Silver, an instructional guide to the silversmith's
art.

     (A Spectrum Book)
     Bibliography: p.
     Includes index.
     1. Silverwork. I. Title.
TS730.R42   739.2'34   80-17705
ISBN   0-13-810218-X
ISBN   0-13-810200-7 (pbk.)

© 1981 by Ruel O. Redinger

A SPECTRUM BOOK

Printed in the United States of America

10 9 8 7 6 5 4 3 2 1

Editorial/production supervision and interior design by Fred Bernardi
Cover design by Honi Werner
Manufacturing buyer: Barbara Frick

PRENTICE-HALL INTERNATIONAL, INC., *London*
PRENTICE-HALL OF AUSTRALIA PTY. LIMITED, *Sydney*
PRENTICE-HALL OF CANADA, LTD., *Toronto*
PRENTICE-HALL OF INDIA PRIVATE LIMITED, *New Delhi*
PRENTICE-HALL OF JAPAN, INC., *Tokyo*
PRENTICE-HALL OF SOUTHEAST ASIA PTE. LTD., *Singapore*
WHITEHALL BOOKS LIMITED, WELLINGTON, *New Zealand*

CONTENTS

PREFACE

This book was written for those who want to work with sterling silver. It contains six basic projects for the beginning silversmith to complete which have been specifically chosen for their simple design, elementary techniques of construction, and merchandising appeal.

Creating these projects is not enough. They must also have consumer appeal, and hence, be marketable. A profit not only insures the necessary money to replenish the silversmith's stock and supplies, but it also signifies general public acceptance, which the beginning silversmith needs to motivate him to continue to develop his talent and his craft.

The six projects were also selected on the basis of the fundamental steps required for work as a silversmith—steps such as basic soldering, cutting, filing, shaping, hammering, and finishing. The use of basic chemicals such as silver solder flux and pickling solutions is also included.

A beginning silversmith should have little or no difficulty in completing each of the six projects if he pays close attention to all the instructions.

Many techniques will be learned upon completion of the first project that can be carried over to the subsequent five projects. This will become very evident as the individual progresses from one project to the next. Therefore, it is important for the beginning silversmith to complete the first project before going on to the second or third project.

It is also equally important for the beginning silversmith to repeat each project more than once before proceeding to the next one. For example, I would suggest that at least two rings be completed in Project 1 before going on to Project 2. By repeating Project 1, the beginning silversmith will develop his own style of basic techniques and shortcuts as he becomes more confident in the basic fundamentals.

In addition, it is very important for the beginning silversmith to pay particular attention to the information on sterling silver, filing, soldering, pickling, and finishing which are covered in the chapters preceding Project 1. This information should be read and completely understood before attempting the first project. All the experiments contained therein should be completed before going any further.

The six projects in this book will give the experience one needs in perfecting his cutting, soldering, filing, shaping, hammering, and finishing techniques. Once you have mastered these six projects you will be ready for more intricate and advanced designs.

Ruel O. Redinger

INTRODUCTION: BECOMING A SILVERSMITH

Crafting with wood, brass, tin, copper, and glass can be interesting and rewarding, but they will never bring you the complete satisfaction of working with sterling silver. Gold and platinum are equally satisfying to work with, but their prohibitive cost is outside the financial reach of the average craftsman and consumer. The cost of more expensive metals also limits the amount of experimentation needed to improve and perfect one's craft. On the other hand, sterling silver, although much less expensive, is intrinsically valuable enough to be coveted by many consumers. In fact, a well-crafted piece of copper or brass jewelry, which may be equal in craftsmanship to sterling silver jewelry, will frequently be rejected by the consumer because of its lower dollar value.

You will feel respect for your silversmith's craft, especially when you witness the large crowds of people who gather at a silversmith's booth at a craft show to watch in fascination as he plies his tools skillfully to produce beautiful pieces of jewelry. Further, creating a valuable piece of jewelry that people will proudly wear is both an exhilarating and personally satisfying experience, and in a sense, your artistry is being applauded each time someone wears one of your creations.

One of your creations presented to a family member or friend can be a gift appreciated both for the painstaking work you have put into it, as well as for its value upon completion, adding to the gift a special significance for those you love.

Handcrafted sterling silver jewelry also has the potential for longevity. Well-made pieces of jewelry have a history of being passed on from generation to generation within a family. Hence, it is possible that your jewelry will exist for many years to come, and even the possibility that a piece of your jewelry may one day become a museum piece. Indeed, well-crafted jewelry of value can be a form of personal immortality—an identity in the future.

Working with sterling silver also commands the personal respect of people in the community. A silversmith becomes part of that community and an authority on all types of jewelry. In a short period of time he will find himself inundated with many questions from people about the value of various jewels or sterling jewelry. As a silversmith's reputation grows throughout his community, people heretofore unknown to him begin to seek his expertise with increasing rapidity.

A silversmith is filled with joy when he creates a piece of jewelry exactly to a consumer's specifications. When a consumer desires a particular type of jewelry that cannot be found in the local retail stores he will seek out the silversmith. Creating the project to your consumer's design is both challenging and fun. You will find it an overwhelming delight to fulfill this need, because the consumer's gratitude is a real tribute to your craft and to you—the artist. Special design in custom silvercrafting is exciting and gives the silversmith a true sense of accomplishment when he has completed the piece of jewelry. It is one of the most stimulating experiences the silversmith will encounter.

As a silversmith gathers more experience, the repair of sterling silver jewelry will be another rewarding phase of silversmithing work. The consumer's sadness when he or she brings in a broken, torn, or shattered piece of jewelry is heartbreaking. It is only with great reluctance that the consumer leaves the broken jewelry in your care—almost as if it were a loved one being left behind. However, his delight upon seeing the jewelry restored to its original excellence is very gratifying to the silversmith. Indeed, the consumer seems to view the silversmith more like a magician rather than as the skilled craftsman he truly is!

In short, I can name no other craft that offers people a project of value that is within their financial reach. In my opinion, no other craft offers the craftsman the opportunity to obtain the personal feelings of need, respect, and admiration from his community. Indeed, there are few crafts that allow a craftsman to create numerous projects that are both an extension of himself and that may well last until the end of time!

I

DEFINING STERLING SILVER

Sterling silver is not pure silver. Pure silver is very soft, but not as soft as gold. It is considered a soft and pliable metal that can be stretched or hammered into an almost translucent state. It is an excellent conductor of heat and electricity, superior to all other metals in that regard. Pure silver is an element listed on the Periodic Element Table as Ag. It contains forty-seven electrons, an atomic weight of 107.870, and a specific gravity of 10.50. Silver is found throughout the world in a pure state and also as a by-product of ores such as copper, zinc, and lead.

Pure silver is not sterling silver. Sterling silver is an alloy made up of 92.5 percent pure silver and 7.5 percent pure copper. The elements of silver and copper have a bonding capability with each other. By adding 7.5 percent copper to pure silver it causes the silver to become less pliable and stronger in its structure. This is a necessary process when silver is fabricated into coins or jewelry.

The specific discovery date of silver is unknown. The use of silver dates back over five thousand years. It has always been used as a decorative metal and at times as the basis for various monetary systems. At one time England used coins with a 92.5 percent pure silver content and termed this percentage *sterling*. Silver has been considered precious for many centuries and will probably continue to be so in the future.

II

SOLDERING STERLING SILVER

Soldering is the most important single skill to develop when working with sterling silver. Only through practice or trial and error can excellence in soldering be developed. Most silversmiths develop their own personal techniques through practice and create a "feel" for the solder and silver that they are working with.

It is important to spend some time in preparing yourself in soldering techniques before attempting the first project. A few hints and exercises follow which you may find helpful in quickly becoming expert in soldering sterling silver.

Three types of silver solder are used when working with sterling silver. They are:

	Melting Point	Flowing Point
1. Hard silver solder	1365°F	1450°F
2. Medium silver solder	1335°F	1390°F
3. Easy silver solder	1280°F	1325°F

As you can see, the difference among these three solders is the melting point and the flowing point. The melting point is reached when the silver solder changes from a solid to a liquid state when heated; the flowing point is reached when the silver solder actually flows or runs when heat is continually applied. In soldering sterling silver we are concerned more with the flowing point than with the melting point.

Another difference among the three types of solder is the

amount of copper and zinc each contains. Hard silver solder is the cleanest solder because it contains less copper and zinc than either the medium or easy solder. Conversely, easy solder is the least pure because it has the highest copper and zinc content. The amount of zinc and copper in silver solder is also the reason for the different melting points among the three types of solder. The more copper and zinc added to the silver, the lower the melting point.

Sterling silver melts at about 1640°F. This is the danger point when fabricating with sterling silver. Many projects have been ruined when the application of heat has allowed the sterling silver to reach the melting point of 1640°F. It stands to reason that when soldering two different pieces of sterling silver together, you must use a solder of less than 1640°F or your project will melt. To further clarify this point, note the flowing points of the three different solders in comparison with the melting point of sterling silver.

	Solder Flowing Point	Difference	S/S Melting Point
Hard solder	1450° F	190° F	1640° F
Medium solder	1390° F	250° F	1640° F
Easy solder	1325° F	315° F	1640° F

As you can see, the safest silver solder to use when soldering sterling silver is easy solder because of its safety tolerance of 315°F. When hard solder is used, the safety tolerance is only 190°F.

It is best for beginners to use easy solder even though it contains more copper and zinc. Then, as you become more adept in your techniques and more confident in your craft, you may move upwards to medium and hard solders.

You should complete the following three experiments before you begin your first project.

EXPERIMENT 1

Items needed: One small piece of hard silver solder
One small piece of medium silver solder
One small piece of easy silver solder

Silver soldering flux
Soldering block
Propane torch

Clean all three pieces of silver solder with light steel wool. Place all three pieces of silver solder on the soldering block in a small circle, about ⅛ inch from each other. Apply silver soldering flux to each piece of solder. Light your propane torch and turn to a medium flame. Apply the flame to the three pieces of solder, rotating the flame in a circular motion in order to heat all three pieces at the same time. Apply the heat until all pieces have melted.

Answer the following three questions:

1. Which piece of solder melted first?
2. Which piece of solder melted second?
3. Which piece of solder melted last?

You should have answered easy silver solder for the first question, medium silver solder for the second, and hard silver solder for the third.

EXPERIMENT 2

Items needed: One small piece of hard solder
One small piece of medium solder
One small piece of easy solder
One small piece of sterling silver
Silver soldering flux
Soldering block
Propane torch

Place all three pieces of clean silver solder, along with the small piece of sterling silver, in a circle approximately ⅛ inch from each other on a soldering block. Apply silver soldering flux to all four pieces. Light the propane torch and turn to a medium to heavy flame. Apply heat to the four pieces in a circular fashion so that all four pieces heat at the same time. Heat until the four pieces melt.

Answer the following four questions:

1. Which piece melted first?
2. Which piece melted second?
3. Which piece melted third?
4. Which piece melted fourth?

You should have answered easy silver solder for the first question, medium silver solder for the second, hard silver solder for the third, and sterling silver for the fourth.

EXPERIMENT 3

Items needed: Two separate small pieces of sterling silver
One small strip of easy silver solder
Silver soldering flux
Soldering block
Propane torch

Make sure that all surfaces of silver and solder are cleaned with light steel wool. Place one piece of the sterling silver on the soldering block. Apply soldering flux. Place the second piece of sterling silver so that both are touching at some point. Place the small piece of silver solder at that seam point at which both pieces of sterling silver meet. Apply silver soldering flux. Light the propane torch and apply a heavy flame to the two pieces of sterling silver, rotating the flame in a circular fashion so that both pieces heat evenly. Apply the flame until the easy silver solder melts and flows into the seam. Quickly remove the flame and turn the torch off. With tweezers, pick up the project and place in water to cool. Examine the seam to see if the two pieces of sterling silver are soldered together.

EXPERIMENT 4

Items needed: Small piece of scrap sterling silver
Silver soldering flux
Soldering block
Propane torch

Place the piece of scrap sterling silver on the soldering block and apply the silver soldering flux. Light the propane torch to a heavy flame. Apply the flame to the piece of sterling silver, rotating the flame in a circular fashion. Observe the color changes in the sterling silver as it is heated. Observe the cherry red color just before it begins to melt, break down, and flow into a small ball. Observe the silver as you continue to apply the heat and note the reactions and motion of the fluid sterling silver.

You have now finished four important experiments that should make you aware of the actions of sterling silver and silver solder. Remember that soldering is the most important part of the silversmith's craft and that personal experiences are the most important in forming techniques for the growth of that craft.

III

FILING
STERLING SILVER

In order to produce superior work expert filing should not be overlooked as an important step to that end. A good silversmith will have available for use different types of files as each occasion requires. The removal of burrs, excess silver, and solder is a continuing objective as he builds his artwork. The smoothing out of various cuts and designs would be next to impossible without the use of differently shaped and sized files.

Most people are familiar with the regular large-size files, such as the flat, round, half-round, three-square, and barrette files used around the home for general filing of coarse metals; however, for more intricate and delicate work, needle files are needed. Needle files are much smaller, approximately five to six inches in length, and have tapered bodies. Some of the most common shapes of needle files include the flat, round, half-round, three-square, knife, square, barrette, marking, equaling, crossing, round-edge joint, and slitting files. The following diagram illustrates the different shapes of the files mentioned above.

THREE SQUARE FILE—Tapered to a point.

SPLITTING FILE—Flat end.

Figure III–1   Diagram of file shapes

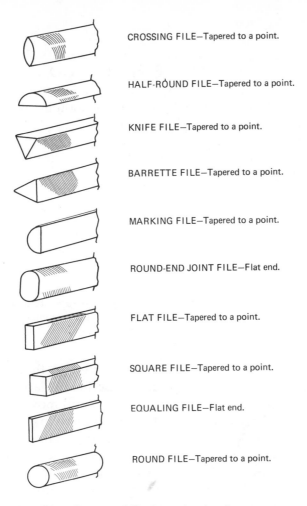

CROSSING FILE—Tapered to a point.

HALF-ROUND FILE—Tapered to a point.

KNIFE FILE—Tapered to a point.

BARRETTE FILE—Tapered to a point.

MARKING FILE—Tapered to a point.

ROUND-END JOINT FILE—Flat end.

FLAT FILE—Tapered to a point.

SQUARE FILE—Tapered to a point.

EQUALING FILE—Flat end.

ROUND FILE—Tapered to a point.

Figure III–1   Diagram of file shapes (*continued*)

I have used all the aforementioned files to complete various projects throughout my career. Eventually, you will also use most of them as you continue to perfect your craft and attempt more complicated designs. Although you will need only a few of the needle files in completing the projects in this book, it would be wise to obtain a complete set of needle files for future use.

As you utilize these different files in your work you will begin to develop the filing techniques that are best suited to you. This is perfectly acceptable; however, I would like to caution against one particular error that some craftsmen make in their filing techniques. When using a file, many beginners make the error of filing a piece of metal with both a forward and backward stroke. This is incorrect. FILE ONLY WITH A FORWARD STROKE! By filing with a forward stroke only, the filing surface of the metal will be much smoother, which will make the completion of the project much easier.

In order that you may better understand the reasoning behind the use of this forward stroke technique, complete the following experiment.

EXPERIMENT

Items needed: Flat needle file

Vise

Three inch piece of eight-gauge sterling silver square wire. (You may substitute a less expensive metal such as brass for this experiment if you desire.)

Place the square wire into the vise so that the end of the square wire is facing upward to be filed. Place the flat needle file on the top end of the square wire and move the file forward and then backward over the metal, applying equal weight to each stroke. Repeat the back and forth filing for at least ten strokes. Remove the file and the piece of square wire from the vise and observe the filed surface.

Return the square wire to the vise with the opposite end facing upward and ready for filing. Using only the forward stroke of your flat needle file, apply at least ten strokes. Remove the square wire and observe the filed surface. Compare the forward only stroke surface with the forward and backward stroked surface on the other end. You will note a much smoother finish on the end at which the forward stroke only was applied.

Continue to experiment with the different shapes of files, comparing the back and forth filing with the forward only filing until you feel you are familiar enough with this procedure and ready to begin filing Project 1.

IV
PICKLING STERLING SILVER

After a high temperature flame is applied to a sterling silver project for the purpose of soldering, a fire scale or copper oxide develops on the surfaces of the sterling silver. If this scale or oxide is not completely removed, your finishing step will be very difficult. It is best to remove this fire scale by soaking the sterling silver in a solution strong enough to complete the job. Some silversmiths use one part sulfuric acid to eight parts water, and soak their projects for about five to ten minutes. Sulfuric acid is a very dangerous chemical and can cause serious burns to you or other members of your household. It is my suggestion that as a beginner you should avoid using this chemical as a pickling solution.

There are much less dangerous commercial pickling agents available at your local supply store. They are effective in removing fire scale even though the process may take a little longer. However, commercial pickling agents are also not without some dangers. They are poisonous and can cause minor skin burns. They can also cause serious injury to your eyes. Whatever commercial pickling agent you purchase, be sure to read the warnings on the package and follow the instructions completely.

It is best to store your prepared pickling solution in a glass container with a glass lid, making sure to label the container as dangerous acid. Use a small plastic tray and plastic tongs when you utilize the solution for pickling your sterling silver projects.

It is very important to wash your project off with water after removing it from the pickling solution. Removing the fire scale from your project by pickling is a very necessary and important step if you expect to obtain a project with a quality finish.

To better understand the effect of pickling solution on sterling silver, complete the following experiment.

EXPERIMENT

Items needed: Three pieces of ½ inch × ½ inch sterling silver sheet
Commercial pickling solution
Silver soldering flux
Soldering block
Plastic tray and plastic tongs
Propane torch

Place all three pieces of sterling silver on a soldering block and apply silver soldering flux to each piece. Heat each piece with your propane torch until the metal begins to turn a cherry red color. Remove the flame and cool in water. Place the three pieces back on the soldering block and repeat this heating process a second time. These two heating applications should build up a considerable amount of fire scale on each piece of sterling silver.

Pour your commercial pickling agent from your glass storage container into your plastic tray and place all three pieces of the sterling silver sheet into the solution. After five minutes has elapsed, remove one piece of the sterling silver sheet from the pickling solution, wash it in water, and dry. After fifteen minutes has passed, remove the second piece of sterling silver sheet from the pickling solution, wash, and dry. At the end of thirty minutes, remove the last piece of sterling silver sheet, wash with water, and dry.

Place all three pieces of sterling silver sheet next to each other and observe the difference among them. Note the difference between the piece you removed from the pickling solution at the five minute mark and the piece you removed at the fifteen minute mark. Compare both these pieces with the piece that was in the pickling solution for thirty minutes.

It should now be obvious to you that the piece of sterling silver sheet that was left in the pickling solution for thirty minutes was free of any fire scale and that its color was much whiter than the other two pieces that were tested. Remember this white color. All of your projects must be pickled to this point if they are to be ready for superior finishing techniques.

V
POLISHING STERLING SILVER

There are many different commercial polishing compounds on the market today that can be purchased and used to buff your completed project to a high luster. These polishing compounds differ primarily in their abrasive ability to remove small layers of metal from a project.

I use two compounds in finishing my projects. In the first step I use tripoli compound, which has the abrasive power not only to dull polish your sterling silver but also to remove scratches and solder which build up on various parts of a project during construction. When using tripoli, however, be careful not to hold your project in the same position for too long. It has such strong abrasive powers that it can easily wear through the sterling silver in a very short time, thus weakening the project's structure.

For the second step in polishing your project, I suggest the use of jeweler's red rouge compound, which is a much milder abrasive than tripoli and will finish off your project to a very high luster.

It should be emphasized that the same buffs are not used for both the tripoli and jeweler's red rouge compounds. Each abrasive compound should have its own buffing wheel. Label your buffs to show a T for tripoli and an R for red rouge so that you will not mistakenly intermix both compounds on the same buff.

To use the polishing compounds, a ⅓ or ½ horsepower electric motor is needed to mount the buffing wheels. A double-ended shaft on the motor is preferable, although a single-ended shaft motor is sufficient; however, frequent changing of the wheels would be necessary in that case. The double-ended shaft motor will accommodate two buffing wheels at a time, separating the red rouge buff on one side and the tripoli buff on the other. To make the changing of buffing wheels less difficult, it would be wise to purchase two tapered spindles that attach to the ends of the motor shafts. One tapered spindle would need a right-hand thread and the other spindle would need a left-hand thread.

For detailed and delicate finishing a flexible shaft machine should be used. This tool is very much like a dentist's drill in that it has a smaller motor with a flexible shaft leading to a small handpiece. It should also have a foot-operated speed control so that different speeds can be attained for any particular type of finshing. A good supply of miniature buffs should be on hand for use in conjunction with tripoli and red rouge compounds.

Finishing your project is an extremely important step in creating fine art and should not be taken casually. Many excellent creations have been ruined by sloppy techniques in the final stages of finishing. To better understand polishing compounds and their abrasive action, complete the following experiment.

EXPERIMENT

Items needed: Two six-inch cotton buffs attached to the shaft of a ⅓ to ½ H.P. motor

Tripoli compound

Red rouge compound

1-inch × 3-inch piece of twenty-six-gauge sterling silver sheet

Turn on your motor, making sure that the buffing wheels are turning downward and away from you, not upward and away from you. Always work on the lower half of the buffing wheel when you are applying abrasive compounds or metal to the buff so that any loose debris will be thrown away from you and not toward you. It would be wise to wear safety glasses during this operation.

Apply tripoli compound to the buff until the buff is saturated with the compound. Holding the 1-inch × 3-inch sterling silver sheet firmly in your hand, press the flat side of the metal gently against the lower half of the buffing wheel, pulling it away periodically to oberve the effect of tripoli compound on the sterling silver. After you have observed the action of the abrasive on the sterling silver and noted the soft finish, turn off the motor. Wipe the sheet clean with a cloth.

Using a different buff, turn on the motor and apply jewler's red rouge. Place the same section of the sterling silver sheet— that was previously buffed by tripoli—against the red rouge buff. Periodically remove the sterling silver sheet and observe the developing high luster produced by the red rouge compound.

The final step of this experiment is to observe the power of the tripoli abrasive in removing layers of stering silver from the sheet. In order to do this, apply the end of the sterling silver sheet to the tripoli buff, allowing the buff to concentrate on one particular portion of the sheet for an extended period of time. Periodically observe the amount and speed in which the tripoli compound removes the layers of sterling silver. Conclude this experiment when you feel that you are knowledgeable about these two abrasives and confident in their use.

VI
CABOCHONS

Selecting a stone for your project depends primarily on each individual's taste. What is delightful to one person may not be exciting to another. There are many differently sized, shaped, and colored stones available to the public to satisfy a wide variety of tastes.

For the projects in this book the beginning silversmith will work with the cabochon. The cabochon is shaped in an oval or round form with a domed top and a flat bottom. For the purpose of creating the projects in this book, we will use only the oval-shaped cabochon in sizes of 12 × 10, 14 × 10, 18 × 13, 25 × 18, and 40 × 30 millimeter. The type of stone and its color will be left to your personal selection.

Cabochons are relatively inexpensive, depending on your choice of stone. Prices on stone vary, depending on the availability and popularity of a particular stone. I have observed turquoise double and triple in price within a twelve-month period because of increased popularity and decreased supply. I have also seen this same turquoise fall backward to its previous low price because its popularity waned and its supply increased. Therefore, if any particular stone is in short supply and difficult for your supplier to obtain, you may be assured that the price of that stone will be considerably higher than that of those stones in good supply.

As a beginning silversmith it would be prudent to obtain those stones that are plentiful and less expensive. As you become more expert in your craft and the chance of ruining your stone lessens, you may then feel sufficiently confident to choose a more expensive stone.

Cabochons are measured in millimeters. (There are twenty-five millimeters to an inch.) The oval cabochon is measured from end to end and side to side. The round cabochon is measured across the diameter only. The following is an example of these measurements on a 25 × 15 millimeter oval and a 20 millimeter round.

Figure VI–1   Millimeter sizes of ovals and rounds

Oval cabochons are generally found at your supplier in sizes from 8 × 6 millimeter up to 30 × 40 millimeter. The most common sizes available are 8 × 6, 10 × 8, 12 × 10, 14 × 10, 16 × 12, 18 × 13, 25 × 18, 30 × 22, and 40 × 30 millimeters. Examples of a few of these sizes follow.

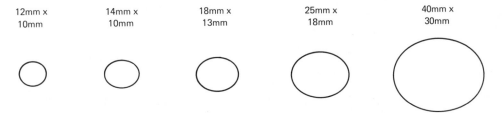

Figure VI–2   Millimeter sizes of oval cabochons

Round cabochons are generally available in all sizes from 4 millimeter up to 22 millimeter in diameter. An example of some of these sizes are shown in the following diagram.

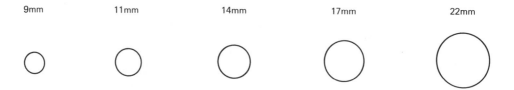

| 9mm | 11mm | 14mm | 17mm | 22mm |

Figure VI–3 Millimeter sizes of round cabochons

The following list is provided to aid you in selecting the type of stone you wish to use for your project. It contains a small selection of those stones that are generally available from your suppliers.

AMAZONITE Light green color.

AVENTURINE Dark green color.

BLOODSTONE Dark green color with red flecks.

BLUE LACE Bluish white color with blue gray stripes.

BLUE LAPIS Dark blue color with gold flecks.

BOTSWANA Brownish gray color with white stripes.

CARNELIAN Clear transparent red or red orange.

CORAL Bright red color.

CRAZY LACE White with a gray to black marble effect.

FIRE AGATE Brown color with transparent orange and yellow.

GOLDSTONE Light brown, blue, or green transparent stone with copper flecks.

GREEN MOSS Medium transparent green with dark green moss effect.

JADE Light to dark solid green.

JET Solid black color.

MALACHITE Light green and dark green marble effect.

ONYX Pure black color or a pure white color.

RHODOCHROSITE Light pink with a dark pink marble effect.

RHODONITE Pink with a black to brown marble effect.

SARDONYX Pink or red color with white stripes.

SNOWFLAKE Solid black color with white flecks.

SODALITE Dark blue color with light blue to white background.

SPECTROLITE Deep dark blue with transparent red, yellow, and green reflections.

TIGER EYE Honey, brown, blue, or red in color with lighter contrasting stripe.

TURQUOISE Deep blue, light blue, or green in color with brown or black matrix.

UNIKITE A medium green color with an orange marble effect.

VII
STERLING SILVER FINDINGS

Figure VII–1 diagrams and names the different types of sterling silver findings that are generally stocked by most suppliers. These are basic sterling silver findings that you will become familiar with as you complete these projects and make progress in this craft.

Figure VII–1 Diagram of sterling silver findings

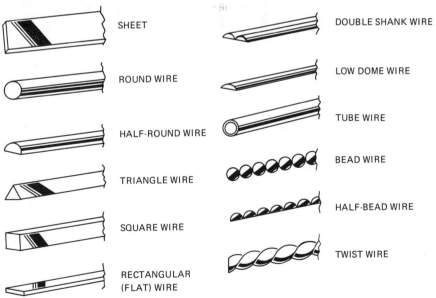

SHEET

DOUBLE SHANK WIRE

ROUND WIRE

LOW DOME WIRE

HALF-ROUND WIRE

TUBE WIRE

TRIANGLE WIRE

BEAD WIRE

SQUARE WIRE

HALF-BEAD WIRE

RECTANGULAR (FLAT) WIRE

TWIST WIRE

VIII

MINIMUM SUPPLIES AND TOOL REQUIREMENTS

Tools and supplies needed for the six projects in this book can be obtained from most lapidary, silver, and jewelry suppliers listed in the yellow pages of your telephone directory (see Silversmith Supplier's List on pages 142–55); if not, they will be able to direct you to the proper sources for obtaining them.

A listing of tools and supplies you will need to complete the experiments and all six projects in this book follows. You may be able to substitute some of the tools and supplies with equipment that you already have at your disposal.

Tools

One small hammer
One ring mandrel with graduated ring sizes
One flint torch lighter
One hand drill
One set of drill bits
One center punch
One bracelet mandrel
One set of small needle files
One rawhide mallet
One jeweler saw with saw blades
One flat-nosed pliers
One round-nosed pliers
One pair of universal shears
One propane torch set with propane tank

One curved burnisher
One jeweler's polishing unit including motor, etc.
One each—left and right tapered spindles for motor shafts
One HANDMADE stamp (Optional)
One STERLING SILVER stamp (Optional)
One finger-size gauge
One optical visor (Focus—10 inch—2 X power)
One pair of curved and serrated pointed tweezers
One plastic acid tray
One pair of plastic acid tongs
One flexible shaft machine
One small soft-haired artist brush
One letter stencil sheet
One cabochon template
One small vise

Supplies

One charcoal block for soldering
Two fire bricks for soldering
Two six-inch cotton polishing buffs
Two inside ring buffs
One package of soldering pins
Two brush wheel buffs
Two two-inch felt crevice buffs with tapered edges
One stick of jeweler's red rouge
One stick of tripoli abrasive compound
One bottle of self-pickling silver soldering flux
One package of pickling solution
One piece of light steel wool
One small piece of emery cloth
One bottle of oxidizing solution
Two commercial spring pins
One commercial watch
One commercial three-link watchband with clasp

Cabochons

One 18mm × 13mm cabochon for the woman's ring
One 25mm × 18mm cabochon for the man's ring
One 40mm × 30mm cabochon for the woman's bracelet

One 18mm × 13mm cabochon for the woman's pendant
Two 12mm × 10mm cabochons for the man's watchband
Two 14mm × 10mm cabochons for the man's watchband

Sterling Silver

2 inches of 18-gauge round wire
12 inches of 10-gauge round wire
12 inches of 8-gauge half-round wire
½ inch of 16-gauge half-round wire
3½ inches of 8-gauge square wire
14 inches of 8-gauge × ⅛-inch flat wire
11 inch × 4 inch 26-gauge sheet
3 inch × 4 inch 24-gauge sheet
3 inch × 4 inch 20-gauge sheet
8 inches of 16-gauge bead wire
4 inches of 14-gauge twist wire
2 inches of 12-gauge (outside diameter) tubing
20 inches of 28-gauge × ⅛-inch plain bezel
½ ounce of hard solder
½ ounce of medium solder
½ ounce of easy solder (Obtain 1½ ounce if you intend to use only easy solder on your projects.)

IX

MAKING
A WOMAN'S RING
Project 1

NOMENCLATURE OF A WOMAN'S RING

Memorize the various parts of the ring listed below before you begin Project 1. Reference to these ring parts is used throughout the instructions.

RING HEAD the section of a ring that includes the bezel, bezel trim, and bezel base

RING SHANK the section of the ring that circles the under part of the finger

BEZEL the part of the ring head that encircles the cabochon

BEZEL TRIM the strip of silver wire that surrounds base of bezel and sits on bezel base; usually, beaded or twist wire is used

BEZEL BASE the platform that the bezel and bezel trim sit upon

CABOCHON the stone that is used to fit inside the bezel

Figure IX–1 Nomenclature of a woman's ring

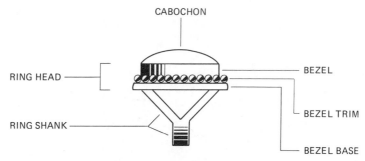

Before you begin this first project, make sure that you have read Chapters I through V on Soldering, Filing, Pickling, and Finishing Sterling Silver, and complete all the experiments contained in those chapters.

If you have already completed the experiment sections, you are now ready to complete your first sterling silver project—a woman's ring. Take your time, read all the instructions completely, and observe all the pictures. The more precisely you follow the instructions in this project, the easier it will be to complete the other projects in this book. Good luck on your first project!

STEP 1. Obtain the following supplies to complete this project: one piece of 1 inch × 1 inch 26-gauge S/S sheet, four inches of 28-gauge × ⅛-inch S/S plain bezel, four inches of 16-gauge S/S bead wire, three inches of 18-gauge × ⅛-inch S/S flat wire, and one 18mm × 13mm cabochon of your choice.

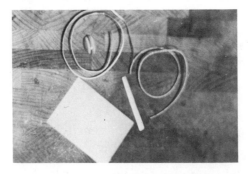

Figure IX–2 Supplies

STEP 2. Obtain your choice of a cabochon to be used in your ring. For this project I have chosen a 18mm × 13mm Sardonyx cabochon. Sardonyx is a type of onyx that has red and white bands and is popular for use in a woman's ring.

Figure IX–3 Cabochon

STEP 3. Using a 28-gauge × ⅛-inch bezel, surround the stone with the bezel as shown. Make sure that the bezel is not too tight or too loose around the stone. (It is better to be too tight than too loose because you can always reduce the size of the cabochon, but you can never enlarge it.)

Figure IX–4 Surrounding cabochon with bezel

STEP 4. When you overlap the butt end of the bezel you will note that it is inside, next to the stone. With a pencil, make a mark on the outside bezel exactly where the butt end is located.

Figure IX–5 Marking bezel for cutting

STEP 5. Remove the bezel from the stone and align the butt end of the bezel with the pencil mark made in STEP 4. Using sharp metal shears, snip the bezel at a point approximately ⅛ inch behind the pencil mark, as shown. Note that you will be cutting through two sections of bezel, so make sure that your cut is straight and not on an angle.

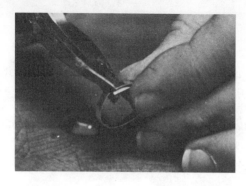

Figure IX–6 Cutting bezel

STEP 6. Take both open ends of the cut bezel and align them perfectly so that both ends butt up against each other as shown.

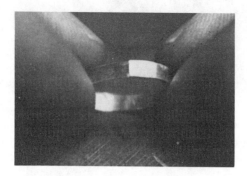

Figure IX–7 Showing bezel seam

STEP 7. When butting both ends of the bezel together in STEP 6, you will discover that the ends do not align perfectly. Use a pair of flat-nosed pliers, as shown, to correct the alignment. (NOTE: Do not become concerned if the bezel loses its original shape at this point. It can be corrected at a later time.)

Figure IX–8 Using flat-nosed pliers on bezel seam

STEP 8. Place the bezel on a soldering block with the seam of the bezel at the top, as shown.

Figure IX–9 Bezel seam

STEP 9. Apply silver soldering flux of your choice to the seam of the bezel. If too much flux is applied, use a small soft-haired artist's brush to remove the excess.

STEP 10. Using HARD Silver Solder, place a small piece on top of the bezel seam. The size of the piece of solder should be just slightly larger than the width and length of the seam. With the silver solder in place you are now ready to solder.

Figure IX–10 Placing solder on bezel seam

STEP 11. Using a propane torch with a heavy nozzle attachment, open the valve slightly to allow a small amount of gas to escape and light the gas with a match or flint torch lighter. Open the valve further to obtain a light flame and apply the flame to the bezel seam with a left to right circular movement so that the bezel will heat evenly. (NOTE: The heat may cause your silver solder to pop off the bezel. If it does pop off, simply replace the solder to the bezel seam, using tweezers, and continue to apply heat.) As you continue to apply heat to the bezel keep your eyes fixed on the silver solder. As soon as the silver solder melts and runs into the seam of the bezel, PULL THE FLAME AWAY FROM THE BEZEL. Do not overburn or you will melt the bezel. Using tweezers, place the hot bezel in water to cool.

STEP 12.   Replace the soldered bezel around the cabochon again to insure proper fit. Using a curved burnisher, reform the bezel to fit the cabochon.

Figure IX–11   Using burnisher on bezel

STEP 13.   With the stone still inside the bezel, place the bezel on top of a light emery cloth. Move the bezel and the stone in a circular back and forth motion to clean the bottom portion of it for future soldering.

Figure IX–12   Cleaning bottom of bezel on emery cloth

STEP 14.   Using a piece of 26-gauge silver sheet, place it on a flat surface and with a piece of fine steel wool, clean the surface of all impurities. With the stone still in the bezel, place it on top of the silver sheet as shown. Use a sharp pencil to outline the bezel, leaving about a ⅛-inch space between the bezel and the pencil mark. (This space outside the bezel will be needed for the bead wire at a later time.) Remove the bezel and stone from the silver sheet and cut out the bezel base with metal shears, carefully following the lines you have drawn. You may find that the silver sheet has become uneven after you have cut out the bezel base. If your silver sheet is uneven and not perfectly flat, place it on a flat surface and use a rawhide mallet to correct the unevenness.

Figure IX–13 Marking the silver sheet around the bezel

STEP 15.   Remove the bezel from the stone, but be careful not to alter the shape of the bezel. Place the bezel on the silver sheet. Make sure that it is properly centered and that the bottom of the bezel meets flush with the silver sheet.

Figure IX–14 Placing bezel on cut out silver sheet

STEP 16.   Place the project on a soldering block as shown.

Figure IX–15 Placing bezel and silver sheet on soldering block

STEP 17.   Apply a few drops of silver soldering flux on the silver sheet, close to the bottom of the bezel. Make sure that the flux covers the whole silver sheet underneath the entire bezel.

Figure IX–16 Applying soldering flux to bezel and silver sheet

STEP 18.   With a pair of tweezers, place two small strips of MEDIUM Silver Solder inside the bezel and at opposite ends, positioning them where the bezel bottom meets the silver sheet. (NOTE: Do not place the solder near the already soldered seam on the bezel. Make sure that you are no closer than 1/4 inch to the bezel seam. Placing your solder near the bezel seam may cause the solder in the bezel seam to bleed, losing all the solder from the previous step as soon as you apply extreme heat.) Check to make sure that the bezel is centered on the silver sheet before soldering.

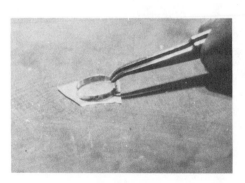

Figure IX–17 Placing solder inside bezel and silver sheet

STEP 19. Light the propane torch and turn the valve to allow a heavy flame. Apply the flame directly above the bezel, following the lines of the bezel in a circular motion. Continue the circular motion until the heat from the flame causes the silver solder to melt and run. As soon as the solder runs, it will follow the base of the bezel all the way around, completing the circle. When the solder has completed this circle, PULL THE FLAME AWAY. Do not overburn or you will melt the bezel and the silver sheet. With tweezers, place the project in water to cool.

STEP 20. Recheck to make sure that the stone fits snugly inside the bezel. If the bezel is too small for the stone, you can start the project over again or, with the use of a grinder or file, reduce the size of the cabochon to fit the bezel.

STEP 21. To form the bezel trim, use a 16-gauge bead wire. Begin to form the wire around the outside of the bezel as shown.

Figure IX–18 Placing bead wire around bezel

STEP 22. Overlap the bead wire as shown and make a pencil mark at the exact point at which you intend to cut. (NOTE: Make sure that the bead wire fits snugly around the bezel before marking with a pencil.)

Figure IX–19 Marking bead wire for cutting

STEP 23. Using metal shears, cut the beaded wire where marked. (NOTE: Be sure not to cut through a bead. Cut in between the beads only.)

Figure IX–20   Cutting bead wire

STEP 24. Take both open ends of the bead wire and butt the ends perfectly together. Place the bead wire on a soldering block and apply one drop of silver soldering flux to the seam. Place a very small dot of MEDIUM Silver Solder on the top of the seam. (NOTE: Too much solder will fill in between the beads and destroy the beaded effect.)

Figure IX–21   Placing solder on bead wire

STEP 25. Light the propane torch and open the valve to give a medium flame. Apply the medium flame to the beaded seam with a back and forth motion until the solder melts and runs. PULL THE FLAME AWAY. Do not overburn or you may melt the bead wire. Cool the project in water.

STEP 26. Place the beaded wire over and around the bezel as shown. Use a curved burnisher to push the bead wire inward and around the bezel into proper position. (NOTE: Make sure that the soldering seam of the bead wire is on the opposite side of the seam of the bezel.)

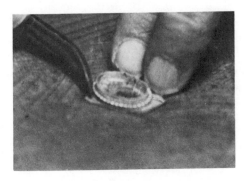

Figure IX–22 Conforming bead wire to bezel with burnisher

STEP 27. Apply silver solder flux to all parts of the bead wire and bezel base as shown.

Figure IX–23 Applying flux to bead wire

STEP 28. Place the project on the soldering block and place four pieces of EASY Silver Solder on the bezel base and against the bead wire. Make sure that the solder is evenly spaced around the bead wire.

Figure IX–24 Placing solder around bead wire and bezel base

STEP 29. Light the propane torch and turn the valve to obtain a heavy flame. Apply the heavy flame to the top of the beaded wire, moving around the wire in a circular motion until you observe the solder break and run inward and under the bead wire toward the bezel. As soon as the last piece of solder breaks and runs, PULL THE FLAME AWAY. Do not overburn or you may melt parts of your project.

STEP 30. Trim the excess silver sheet away from the outside of the bead wire as shown.

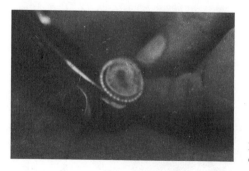

Figure IX–25 Trimming away excess silver sheet

STEP 31. Use a small flat needle file to smooth out the rough edges caused by the trimming in the previous step.

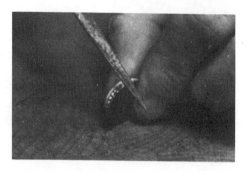

Figure IX–26 Filing bezel base with needle file

STEP 32.   Check the bottom part of the bezel base to make sure that it is smooth and conforms to the shape of the bead wire.

Figure IX–27 Showing bottom of bezel base as it conforms to bead wire

STEP 33.   When making the ring shank, use a strip of 18-gauge × ⅛-inch wide × 1¾ inches in length of flat wire. This length may be used to make a five to seven finger size ring. With a pencil draw a straight line down the middle of the flat wire, about ½ inch in from each side as shown.

Figure IX–28 Marking flat wire with pencil

STEP 34.   Using metal shears, cut inward ½ inch from the end, following the lines you have drawn in the previous step. Make sure that you cut in the middle of the flat wire and not off-center. (NOTE: As you cut you will note that the ends tend to curl upwards and outwards forming a Y shape. Use a flat needle file to file away all marks made from the cutting.)

Figure IX–29 Cutting flat wire on marked pencil line

STEP 35. Place the ring shank on a flat surface and tap lightly with a rawhide mallet to flatten. Turn the ring shank over on its other side and flatten.

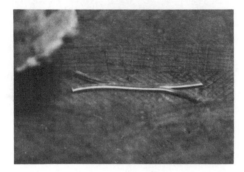

Figure IX–30 Flattening ring shank with rawhide mallet

STEP 36. Using a flat tool of your choice, separate the split ends of the ring shank evenly. Check the width of the ring shank ends against the length of the bezel base to make sure that the width of the shank ends is no wider than the length of the bezel base.

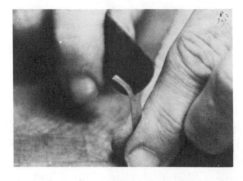

Figure IX–31 Spreading ends of shank evenly

STEP 37. Place the ring shank on a ring mandrel and with your hands, force the ring shank around the mandrel, as shown.

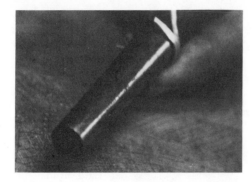

Figure IX–32 Forcing ring shank around mandrel by hand

STEP 38. Continue to force the ring shank around the ring mandrel with the use of a rawhide mallet. Reverse the ring on the mandrel occasionally so that the ring shank will have equal conformity.

Figure IX–33 Forcing ring shank around mandrel with rawhide mallet

STEP 39. Move the ring shank up and down the ring mandrel until you obtain the ring size desired. Then remove the ring from the ring mandrel and use a small flat needle file to smooth out any imperfections caused by shaping.

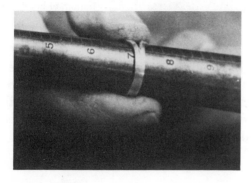

Figure IX–34 Sizing ring shank on mandrel

STEP 40.   Continue to use a flat needle file, filing the ends of the ring shank flat so that they will rest evenly when all four points are placed on the back of the bezel base.

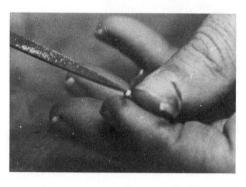

Figure IX–35   Filing ends of the ring shank flat

STEP 41.   Turn the ring head over, so that the bottom of the bezel base is facing upward as shown. Clean the bottom of the bezel base with light steel wool and apply silver soldering flux to the entire bottom.

Figure IX–36   Applying flux to bottom of bezel base

STEP 42.   With the ring head on the soldering block and the bottom of the bezel base up, place the ring shank on the back of the bezel base as shown. Make sure that all four ends of the ring shank set flush against the bottom of the bezel base. Center the ring shank on all sides.

Figure IX–37 Placing ring shank on bottom of bezel base

STEP 43. Using EASY Silver Solder, place a small piece of solder at the base of each of the four ends of the ring shank where they meet the bezel base, as shown.

Figure IX–38 Placing solder where shank meets bezel base

STEP 44. Light the propane torch and turn the valve to obtain a heavy flame. Apply the heavy flame to the project in a circular fashion, concentrating the flame primarily on the bezel base rather than on the ring shank. When you see the last silver solder melt and run under the ring shank, PULL THE FLAME AWAY. Do not overburn or you may melt the ring shank or bezel base. Place the project in water to cool.

STEP 45. (NOTE: The next three steps are optional. If you do not have a HANDMADE or STERLING stamp, skip these few steps and go on to Step 49.) If you do have these stamps, obtain two or three inches of plain 28-gauge × ⅛-inch bezel and lay it down on a hard, flat surface. Place the HANDMADE or STERLING stamp exactly in the middle of the bezel. Using a hammer, deliver one blow directly to the top of the stamp. The blow should be firm but not too hard. (This step may take a little practice before you become expert at it.) After hitting the top of the stamp, check the silver strip to see if HANDMADE or STERLING imprints are clear and even as shown. Using metal shears, cut the silver strip on both sides of each word, allowing about a 1/16-inch space on each side of the word.

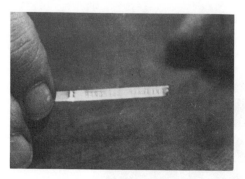

Figure IX–39   Showing silver strip with handmade indentation

STEP 46.   Brush the bottom of the bezel base with the light steel wool. Apply silver soldering flux to the bottom of the bezel base and to the bottom side of the stamped bezel strips.

STEP 47.   Place both the HANDMADE and STERLING strips in the position shown. Place one small dot of EASY Silver Solder next to each of the strips.

Figure IX–40   Placing silver strips on back of bezel base

STEP 48. Light the propane torch and turn the valve to obtain a heavy flame. Apply the heavy flame to the bottom of the bezel base and move the flame using a circular motion and concentrating primarily on the bezel base rather than on the ring shank. As soon as you see the solder melt and run under the stamped strips, PULL THE FLAME AWAY. Do not overburn or you may melt your project. Place the project in water to cool.

STEP 49. Place the completed ring in a safe commercial pickling solution to remove all the fire scale that has accumulated on the sterling silver from heating. Leave the ring in the pickling bath for about half an hour or until all the fire scale is removed and the ring appears white in color. Remove from the pickling solution, rinse in water, and dry.

Figure IX–41   Removing ring from pickling solution

STEP 50. Insert your cabochon inside the bezel. Center the stone and hold it in place with your thumb. Using a curved burnisher, begin to push inward on the bezel with a sliding motion. (IMPORTANT NOTE: Always start pushing in on the bezel at the short curved end before you begin pushing inward on the sides. This will prevent your bezel from crimping on the short curved ends.)

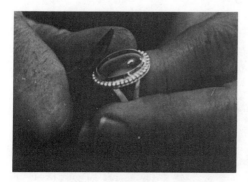

Figure IX–42   Using burnisher on short end of bezel

STEP 51. Still using the curved burnisher, push inward on the sides of the bezel, remembering to use a sliding motion.

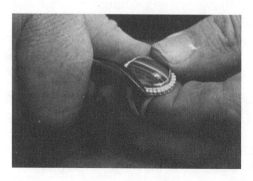

Figure IX–43 Using burnisher on the side portion of bezel

STEP 52. Go back to the point at which you first started to push inward on the bezel with your curved burnisher and begin to push the upper portion of the bezel downward toward the stone, still using a sliding motion. Continue to work first from the short curved ends and then from the sides until the entire bezel is firmly pressed against the cabochon.

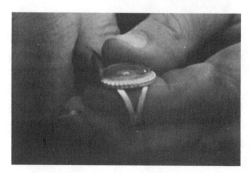

Figure IX–44 Using burnisher to push bezel down onto cabochon

STEP 53. Check your ring to make sure it looks similar to the ring shown.

Figure IX–45 Ring

STEP 54.   Using a flexible shaft machine, insert a felt crevice buff as shown. Apply tripoli abrasive compound to the tapered buff to facilitate the rough finishing of the ring.

Figure IX–46 Tapered buff

STEP 55.   Apply the sharp edge of the tapered buff to the soldered seam of the bezel with a back and forth motion until the seam is eliminated. Continue to use the sharp edge of the tapered buff to smooth out the rest of the bezel.

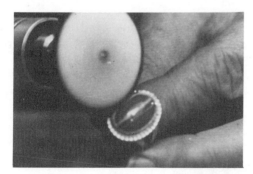

Figure IX–47 Using tapered buff on side of bezel

STEP 56.   Use the crevice buff to smooth out other difficult to reach places on the ring.

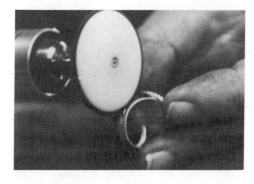

Figure IX–48 Using tapered buff on ring shank

STEP 57.   Use an electric motor with double shafts for this step. Place tapered spindles on both motor shafts. Place a ring buff on one of the tapered spindles and apply tripoli compound. Place the ring over the ring buff as shown and begin to smooth out the inside of the ring shank. Be careful not to destroy any letter stamping that you placed inside the ring. Reverse the ring on the ring buff to obtain an even finish.

Figure IX–49   Buffing inside ring with tripoli ring buff

STEP 58.   Place a brush wheel buff on one of the tapered spindles and apply tripoli compound to the wheel. Use the brush wheel to get at difficult places such as between the bezel and the bead wire or the bezel base and the ring shank.

Figure IX–50   Buffing ring with tripoli brush wheel

STEP 59.   Attach a cotton buff to one of the tapered spindles and apply tripoli compound. Smooth out all other rough areas on the ring.

Figure IX–51 Buffing ring with tripoli cotton buff

STEP 60.   When Step 59 has been completed, wash the ring in a water and detergent mixture, using a toothbrush to get at small places. Rinse in clear water and dry. (NOTE: If cleaning is difficult because of the buildup of tripoli compound, add a few drops of ammonia to the water and detergent.)

STEP 61.   Attach a ring buff to a tapered spindle and apply jeweler's red rouge compound. Place your ring on the ring buff and polish the inside of the ring to a high luster.

Figure IX–52 Buffing ring on red rouge ring buff

STEP 62.   Attach a brush wheel buff to one of the tapered spindles and apply jeweler's red rouge. Use the brush wheel to get at difficult places just as you did with the tripoli brush wheel and polish to a high luster.

Figure IX–53 Buffing ring on red rouge brush buff

STEP 63. Attach a cotton buff to one of the tapered spindles and apply jeweler's red rouge. Finish off all other parts of the ring to a high luster.

Figure IX–54 Buffing ring on red rouge cotton buff

STEP 64. A front view of the finished woman's ring.

Figure IX–55

STEP 65.   A side view of the finished woman's ring.

Figure IX–56

STEP 66.   A top view of the finished woman's ring.

Figure IX–57

X

MAKING
A MAN'S RING
Project 2

In creating a man's ring, keep in mind that the construction is basically the same as for a woman's ring, that is, it has a bezel, bezel base, bezel trim, ring shank, and cabochon. However, there are three basic differences between the man's ring and the woman's ring. First, the shank is much larger and solid; second, the cabochon is much larger; and third, the bead wire is replaced by twist wire as bezel trim.

The construction of the bezel, bezel trim, and bezel base are accomplished in the same manner as for the woman's ring. If you are in doubt regarding these steps, it would be wise to refer to and review those sections in Project 1. In this project we will spend significantly more time on the construction of the ring shank than on the ring head. Good luck!

STEP 1. The following supplies are needed for this project. 1-inch × 1 ½-inch piece of 26-gauge S/S sheet, 1-inch × 3-inch piece of 26-gauge S/S sheet, six inches of 18-gauge × ⅛-inch of S/S flat wire, four inches of 14-gauge S/S twist wire, 4 inches of 28-gauge × ⅛-inch of S/S plain bezel, and a 25mm × 18mm cabochon of your choice. I will be using a tiger-eye cabochon.

Figure X–1 Supplies

STEP 2. Place your cabochon on a flat surface and surround the cabochon with the 28-gauge × ⅛-inch bezel, making sure that the bezel fit is firm. Mark the bezel with a pencil where it overlaps the butt end as you did in Project 1 and as shown here.

Figure X–2 Marking bezel with pencil

STEP 3. Make sure that the butt ends are clean and align them perfectly end to end. Place the enclosed bezel on a soldering block as shown; apply silver soldering flux and a small piece of HARD Silver Solder across the seam. Solder the seam as you were instructed in Project 1.

Figure X–3 Solder placed on bezel seam

STEP 4. Place your cabochon on the inside of the bezel to ensure a good fit. With your curved burnisher, align the bezel so that it is pressed evenly around the cabochon. With the cabochon still inside the bezel, gently rotate them both on emery cloth, as shown, to clean the bottom portion of the bezel for soldering.

Figure X–4 Cleaning bottom of bezel on emery cloth

STEP 5. Place the bezel on top of the 26-gauge silver sheet for soldering. Be sure that the silver sheet has been cleaned with light steel wool. Apply silver soldering flux and four small pieces of MEDIUM Silver Solder inside the bezel, remembering not to place any solder near the soldered bezel seam.

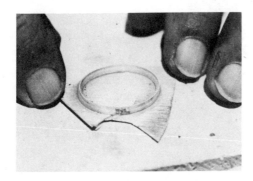

Figure X–5 Placing bezel on top of silver sheet

STEP 6. Using a heavy flame from your propane torch, move in a circular fashion around the bezel and bezel base until the solder breaks and runs completely round the bezel base and bezel. (NOTE: Because of the larger-sized bezel you should increase the circular speed of the flame from your propane torch so that heating remains uniform. Remember not to overburn while soldering.) After this has been done, cool in water.

STEP 7. Surround the bezel with 14-gauge twist wire—sometimes referred to as rope wire—for bezel trim. Mark with a pencil, as shown, and cut the twist wire where it overlaps the butt end, as you did with the bead wire in Project 1.

Figure X–6 Marking twist wire with pencil for cutting

STEP 8. Make sure that the ends are cleaned with steel wool, then butt both ends of the twist wire together. Apply silver soldering flux to the seam where both ends meet. Place a small dot of MEDIUM Silver Solder on the seam, and solder with a medium flame from your propane torch. Cool in water. (NOTE: Using too much solder on the seam will cause the grooves in the twist wire to fill up with solder and destroy the roping effect.)

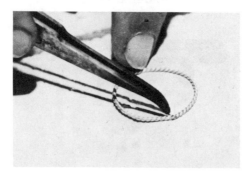

Figure X–7 Placing solder on twist wire seam

STEP 9. Place the soldered twist wire around the bezel to ensure a good fit. Press on the twist wire with your curved burnisher to correct the alignment of the twist wire so that it fits evenly around the bezel. (NOTE: The twist wire seam should not be near the bezel seam.)

Figure X–8 Using burnisher to conform twist to bezel shape

STEP 10.   Apply silver soldering flux around the bezel base and the twist wire. Place four equally separated pieces of MEDIUM Silver Solder on the bezel base next to the twist wire, as shown.

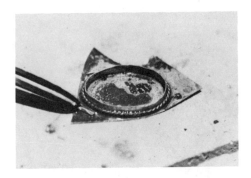

Figure X–9   Placing solder on silver sheet and twist wire

STEP 11.   In a circular motion, apply a heavy flame from your propane torch until you observe the solder break and flow under the twist wire and toward the bezel. Cool in water.

STEP 12.   Check to see that the twist wire is secured to the bezel base by solder at all four points. Trim the excess silver sheet away as shown.

Figure X–10   Trimming excess silver away from bezel base

STEP 13.   File all the outside edges of the bezel base with a flat file so that all edges are smooth and free of burrs. Place the cabochon inside the bezel to check for a good fit.

STEP 14.   Using two pieces of 18-gauge × ⅛-inch flat wire, each piece 2¾ inches in length, lay them on a flat surface and bend each piece into a slight concave shape as shown. Place both pieces of flat wire next to each other so that they bend away from each other as shown. Approximately ½ inch of both center pieces of flat wire should be touching each other as shown.

Figure X–11 Flat wire touching in center

STEP 15. Clean the sections on each piece of flat wire that touch each other with light steel wool. Place the two pieces on a soldering block as shown. Apply silver soldering flux to the seam. Place a medium-sized piece of HARD Silver Solder on the seam as shown.

Figure X–12 Placing solder on flat wire

STEP 16. Apply a heavy flame from your propane torch, moving it up and down the full length of the flat wires to heat all the metal evenly until the solder melts and runs into the groove between both pieces of flat wire. Cool in water.

STEP 17. Your flat wires should be joined together and appear similar to the photograph shown.

Figure X-13 Soldered flat wire

STEP 18. Using a flat tool of your choice, spread the ends of the flat wires wide enough to fit the bottom of the bezel base as shown. Do not spread the ends too far apart and make sure that the bezel base will cover the ends so they cannot be seen when they are soldered to the bezel base. Repeat the same steps to the other ends of the flat wires. Be sure that the opposite ends are spread exactly the same distance apart. If the flat wires lose their shape during this process, straighten them with a rawhide mallet.

Figure X-14 Spreading flat wire to fit bottom of bezel base

STEP 19. Place the flat wire on the top of the 26-gauge silver sheet and with a pencil outline the outside of the flat wire on the silver sheet as shown.

Figure X-15 Outlining flat wire on silver sheet with pencil

STEP 20.   Using metal shears, cut out the form drawn on the silver sheet, staying about ¹⁄₁₆ inch outside the drawn lines. This ¹⁄₁₆ inch will act as an outside platform for placing your solder at a later time.

STEP 21.   Be sure that your silver sheet is perfectly flat and has been cleaned with light steel wool. Check the flat wires to make sure they are also flat and clean them with light steel wool. Place the flat wires on the sheet as shown and check alignment.

Figure X–16   Aligning flat wire on silver sheet

STEP 22.   Apply silver soldering flux to the entire surface of the silver sheet and to the bottom portion of the flat wires that will lay against the silver sheet. Make sure that the flat wires are positioned on the silver sheet so as to allow a small ledge of silver sheet on the outside of the flat wire. Place three large pieces of HARD Silver Solder on the outside ledge of each side as shown. (NOTE: Do not be concerned about the amount of solder you use in this step. There must be enough solder to sufficiently seal all the flat wire to the silver sheet.)

Figure X–17   Placing solder on flat wire and silver sheet

STEP 23.   Use a heavy flame from your propane torch, working it in a circular motion, up and down the full length of the project. When you observe the silver solder melt and run under the flat wire at all points, continue applying the flame for a few seconds more to make sure that a good seal has taken place between the flat wire and the silver sheet. However, be careful not to melt the project. Cool in water.

STEP 24.   With your metal shears, trim off all excess silver plate outside the flat wire and even off the ends. Use a flat file on all the outside edges, filing deep enough so that the outside seam line between the flat wire and the silver sheet is no longer visible.

STEP 25.   Your ring shank should now be similar to the photograph shown.

Figure X–18   Soldered flat wire to silver sheet

STEP 26.   To curve your ring shank to the size you desire, place the ring shank around the ring mandrel and with your fingers, force it around the larger end of the ring mandrel as much as physically possible.

Figure X–19   Forming shank around mandrel with hands

STEP 27. Use the rawhide mallet to continue forcing the ring shank around the mandrel, moving it slowly down toward the smaller end of the mandrel. To obtain the exact size, continue to use the rawhide mallet to force the ring shank to the needed size number on the mandrel. If the ends of the ring shank overlap at this point, remove the ring shank from the mandrel and trim the ends with your metal shears to maintain a spacing between the ends. An acceptable space between the ends of the ring shank is ¼ inch; however, it could be slightly smaller or larger, provided that it fits the bottom part of the bezel base. Continue to use the rawhide mallet in forming your ring shank to the desired size, occasionally reversing the ring shank on the ring mandrel.

Figure X–20 Forcing shank around mandrel, using rawhide mallet

STEP 28. With the ring shank still on the ring mandrel, file the open ends of the flat wire so that they are flat and even with the silver sheet. The purpose of this step is to allow the ring shank ends to fit flush against the bezel base for soldering.

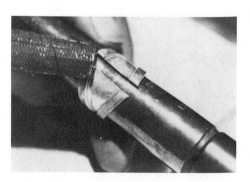

Figure X–21 Filing end portion of ring shank

Making a Man's Ring: Project 2

STEP 29.   Your ring shank should now appear similar to the photograph shown.

Figure X–22   Ring shank

STEP 30.   Place the bezel base on the soldering block so that the bottom side of the bezel base is facing upward. Place the ring shank ends evenly on the bezel base bottom as shown. Make sure that the ring shank is centered perfectly on the bezel base and that the ends of the ring shank fit flush against the bezel base.

Figure X–23   Centering ring shank on back of bezel base

STEP 31.   Apply silver soldering flux to the section where the ring shank ends touch the bezel base. Place two pieces of EASY Silver Solder on each side of the ring shank ends where they touch the bezel base.

STEP 32.   Using your propane torch, apply a heavy flame to the project, remembering to move in a circular motion. Concentrate the flame on the bezel base and the ring shank ends. When you observe the solder melt and run under the ring shank ends, PULL THE FLAME AWAY. Cool in water.

STEP 33.   Your project should now appear similar to the photograph shown. (NOTE: If you have a stamp to apply to the ring, you would now solder the HANDMADE or STERLING stamp to your project, following the instructions used in Project 1.) If you do not have any stamps to apply, place your entire project in a pickling solution for about thirty minutes or until all the fire scale is removed and the sterling silver turns to a pure white color.

Figure X–24   Soldered ring shank and bezel head

STEP 34.   Remove your project from the pickling solution, rinse with water, and dry. Place your cabochon into the inside of the bezel of the ring for proper alignment before setting the stone.

Figure X–25   Placing cabochon inside bezel

STEP 35.   With your curved burnisher, force the bezel inwards toward the cabochon, working from the smaller curved ends first and the sides second, as you learned in Project 1.

Figure X–26 Using burnisher on bezel

STEP 36. When you are finished enclosing the cabochon inside the bezel, polish the ring with tripoli and jeweler's red rouge compound as you did in Project 1.

STEP 37. Front view of the finished man's ring.

Figure X–27

STEP 38. Top view of the finished man's ring.

Figure X–28

STEP 39.   Side view of the finished man's ring.

Figure X–29

XI

MAKING A WOMAN'S BRACELET

Project 3

NOMENCLATURE OF A BRACELET

Memorize the various parts of the bracelet listed below before you begin this project. Use of this terminology will be made throughout this project.

BRACELET HEAD the section of the bracelet head that includes the bezel base, bezel trim, and the bezel.

BRACELET SHANK the section of the bracelet that surrounds the arm or the wrist

BEZEL the part of the ring that encircles the cabochon

BEZEL TRIM the strip of silver wire that surrounds the base of the bezel and sits on the bezel base

BEZEL BASE the platform that the bezel and bezel trim sit upon

CABOCHON the stone that is used to fit inside the bezel

Figure XI–1 Nomenclature of a woman's bracelet

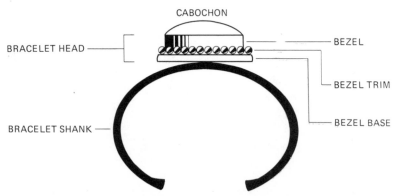

The aim of this project is to familiarize you with the basic two-step procedure of forming a bracelet head and a bracelet shank. These basic steps will give you the background for creating even more complicated bracelets, should you desire to do so.

Making the bracelet head in this project requires the same procedure used in Projects 1 and 2. The only difference is the use of a 40mm × 30mm cabochon, which is a much larger stone; hence, you will need a much larger bezel than you have used before. Remember to use the good soldering techniques that you have developed in Projects 1 and 2. Good luck!

STEP 1.   For this project you will need the following supplies: eleven inches of 8-gauge S/S half-round wire, a two-inch × 1½-inch piece of 26-gauge S/S sheet, five inches of 16-gauge S/S bead wire, five inches of 28-gauge × ⅛-inch S/S plain bezel, one piece of ¾ × ½-inch 20-gauge S/S sheet, and one 40mm × 30mm cabochon of your choice. I will be using a tiger eye cabochon.

Figure XI–2 Supplies

STEP 2.   Enclose your 40mm × 30mm cabochon with 28-gauge × ⅛-inch plain bezel, making sure that it firmly surrounds the cabochon. Mark with a pencil the point at which the bezel overlaps the butt end and cut with metal shears as you did in Project 1.

Figure XI–3 Marking bezel for cutting

STEP 3. Butt both ends of the bezel against each other and place the bezel on the soldering block. Apply silver soldering flux and a small piece of HARD Silver Solder to the seam of the bezel.

Figure XI–4   Placing solder on bezel seam

STEP 4. Use a medium-sized flame from your propane torch and move the flame in a circular motion until the silver solder melts and runs into the seam. Cool in water.

STEP 5. Place the cabochon inside the bezel and place the project on a flat surface. Using your curved burnisher, align the bezel to the cabochon, making sure that all sides are evenly spaced around the stone as shown.

Figure XI–5   Using burnisher to form bezel for cabochon

STEP 6. Place the cabochon and the bezel together on a piece of emery cloth and rotate them to clean the bottom of the bezel for soldering.

STEP 7. Remove the cabochon from the bezel, being careful not to accidentally bend the bezel out of shape, and place it on a clean

26-gauge silver sheet as shown. Apply silver soldering flux around the bottom of the bezel and place four medium-sized pieces of MEDIUM Silver Solder on the bezel base, next to the bezel. Remember not to place the solder near the presoldered bezel seam.

Figure XI–6 Placing solder inside bezel on silver sheet

STEP 8. Use a heavy flame from your propane torch and apply the flame in a rapid circular motion around the bezel and bezel base until the solder melts and flows completely around the bezel and bezel base. Cool in water.

STEP 9. Surround the bezel with 16-gauge bead wire for bezel trim as shown. Mark the bead wire at the point at which it overlaps the butt end and cut at this point. Cut *only* in between the beads.

Figure XI–7 Forming bead wire around bezel

STEP 10. Apply silver soldering flux to the butt ends. Place a dot of MEDIUM Silver Solder on the seam between the two butt ends.

Apply a medium flame from your propane torch to the seam until the solder melts and runs into the seam. Cool in water.

STEP 11.   Place the soldered bead wire over and around the bezel so that it rests on the bezel base. Use your curved burnisher to align the bead wire so that it is even on all sides. Apply silver soldering flux to the bead wire and bezel base. Place four pieces of MEDIUM Silver Solder on the bezel base and next to the bead wire as shown.

Figure XI–8   Placing solder on sheet and bead wire

STEP 12.   Apply a heavy flame from your propane torch to the project, moving the flame in a rapid circular motion, following the bead wire until you see the solder melt and flow under the bead wire and inward toward the bezel. REMOVE THE FLAME IMMEDI-ATELY so that you do not overburn and melt the project. Cool the project in water and dry.

STEP 13.   Trim off all the excess silver sheet outside the bead wire and smooth the rough edges with a file as you did in Project 1. Place the cabochon inside the bezel to check for fit.

STEP 14.   Snip off two 5½-inch pieces of 8-gauge half-round wire. In producing a bracelet shank, it is necessary that these two pieces of 8-gauge half-round wire be flat and straight. Also cut two pieces of ½-inch × ⅜-inch each of 20-gauge silver sheet to use as end plates in soldering the ends of the two pieces of 8-gauge half-round wire. After cleaning all parts with light steel wool, place the two pieces of 5½-inch 8-gauge half-round on top of the two pieces of ½-inch × ⅜-inch silver sheet, utilizing these small silver sheet pieces as end plates, as shown. The spacing between the two parallel half-round wires can be anywhere from $^1/_{16}$ inch up to $^1/_4$ inch, depending on your personal choice. Apply silver soldering flux to both end plates that are to be soldered to the two 8-gauge half-round wires. Place a large piece of HARD Silver Solder to the four points at which the half-round wire lays on the end plates.

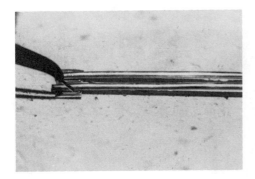

Figure XI–9   Placing solder on end plates

STEP 15.   With your project on the soldering block as shown, you are now ready to solder both ends of the 8-gauge wire to the end plates. Use a heavy flame with your propane torch and apply the heat evenly over the entire project, moving the flame back and forth over its full length until it begins to turn a cherry red directly under the flame. At this time, move the flame to one end of the project, and concentrate it on the end plate using a circular motion until the silver solder melts and flows under the half-round wire. Move quickly to the other end and duplicate the heating technique until the solder melts and flows under the half-round wire at that end. Cool the project in water.

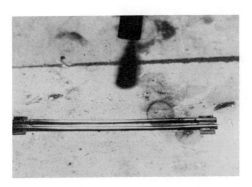

Figure XI–10   Soldering bracelet shank

STEP 16. Smooth and shape the ends of the bracelet shank with a half-round and flat needle files. Round off all the square corners so that the seam between the 8-gauge half-round wire and the small end plates is removed. The object of this filing is to make the end pieces and the half-round wire look as if they were one piece.

Figure XI–11 Filing bracelet shank

STEP 17. With the bracelet shank on a flat surface, flat side down, place your 40mm × 30mm cabochon exactly in the middle of the bracelet shank as shown. With a pencil, mark the position of the cabochon on the bracelet shank. Remove the cabochon and using your hands, spread, at the center, the parallel half-round wires away from each other. The distance you spread these wires apart from each other should not exceed the size of the cabochon. As you spread the half-round wire apart the whole project will have a tendency to twist and turn. Use a rawhide mallet on a flat surface to realign the project.

Figure XI–12 Placing cabochon in center of bracelet shank

STEP 18.   After completing the above step, your project should be similar to the picture shown. Check the width of the spread of the half-round wire with the cabochon as shown to make sure that the distance is not larger than the length of the cabochon.

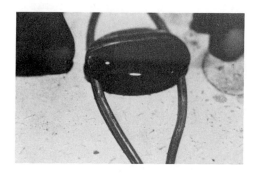

Figure XI–13 Spreading bracelet shank to width of cabochon

STEP 19.   Use 8-gauge half-round wire for a cross piece as shown. Measure and mark the cross piece. Be sure that its location is no further than ½ inch away from a point nearest the cabochon. You will note that the lines of the bracelet shank are on an angle which will also require you to cut the cross piece on an angle. Using a jeweler's saw, cut the cross piece as measured. Place it into the bracelet shank to check the fit. Use a flat needle file to correct any alignment as is necessary. Using the same method as detailed above, make a second cross piece for the other side of the bracelet shank. Make sure that the distance from the cabochon on the second cross piece is the same as that on the first, and also that the distance from the ends of the bracelet shank are equal.

Figure XI–14 Placing cross piece between bracelet shank wires

STEP 20.   Place the bracelet shank on a soldering block and position the cross pieces, making sure that the ends of the cross pieces are in contact with the half-round wire. Be sure that all parts to be soldered are cleaned with light steel wool. Apply silver soldering flux to all four seams to be soldered. Apply a medium-sized piece of MEDIUM Silver Solder to all four seams to be soldered.

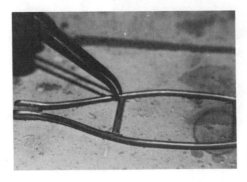

Figure XI–15   Placing solder on cross piece seam

STEP 21.   Use a heavy flame from your propane torch, heating each joint by moving in a circular motion until the solder melts and flows into the seam. When finished with all four seams, cool the project in water.

STEP 22.   Using a small half-round needle file, smooth each joint until the seams cannot be seen and give the appearance of being one piece.

Figure XI–16   Filing cross piece seam

STEP 23.   Place the bracelet shank on a bracelet mandrel and force the bracelet shank around the largest portion of the bracelet mandrel, utilizing a rawhide mallet when necessary as shown. Change positions on the bracelet mandrel to obtain the size you desire and to maintain uniformity.

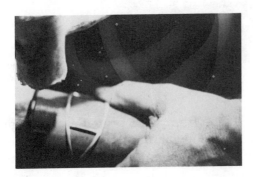

Figure XI–17   Forming bracelet shank to bracelet mandrel with rawhide mallet

STEP 24.   After you have completed shaping your bracelet shank on the bracelet mandrel, it should look similar to the picture shown.

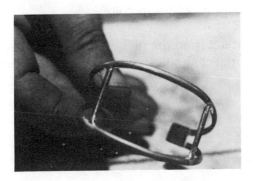

Figure XI–18   Shaped bracelet shank

STEP 25.   Place the bezel head on a soldering block with the bottom of the bezel base facing upward. Place the bracelet shank on top of the bezel base bottom as shown. Make sure that the points of contact between the bracelet shank and bezel base are cleaned with light steel wool. Center the bracelet shank evenly on all sides and apply silver soldering flux to the two seams to be soldered. Place a medium-sized piece of EASY Silver Solder on the bezel base, next to the bracelet shank as shown. Do the same thing on the other seam where the bracelet shank meets the bezel base.

Figure XI–19 Placing bracelet
shank on back of cabochon base

STEP 26. Using a heavy flame from your propane torch, apply the flame
to each seam in a circular motion until the solder melts and
flows under the bracelet shank. Cool the project in water.

STEP 27. If you have stamped lettering strips to apply, it would be now
that you would solder them to the project, following the steps
covered in Project 1. If you do not have stamped lettering strips
to apply, place the project in pickling solution for approximately
thirty minutes or until all the fire scale is removed and the
bracelet appears pure white in color.

STEP 28. Remove the bracelet from the pickling solution, rinse with water,
and dry. Your project should now look similar to the photograph
shown.

Figure XI–20 Soldered bracelet
shank and bracelet head

STEP 29. Place your 40mm × 30mm cabochon inside the bezel and with
the aid of a curved burnisher, compress the bezel around the
cabochon. Remember to start on the short curved ends of the
bezel first to avoid crimping of the bezel.

Figure XI–21 Using burnisher on bezel

STEP 30. Continue to use the curved burnisher in pressing inward on the sides of the bezel as shown. Return to the short curved end of the bezel and press downward on the top of the bezel, making a good seal between the bezel top and the cabochon. Repeat this step on the sides of the bezel. With the knowledge you acquired in Projects 1 and 2, finish the bracelet using tripoli and jeweler's red rouge abrasive compounds to achieve a high luster.

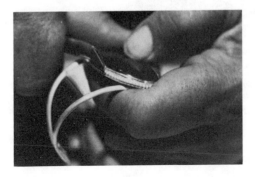

Figure XI–22 Using burnisher on bezel

STEP 31. Front view of the finished woman's bracelet.

Figure XI–23

STEP 32. Top view of the finished woman's bracelet.

Figure XI–24

STEP 33. Side view of the finished woman's bracelet.

Figure XI–25

XII
MAKING
A MAN'S
WATCHBAND
Project 4

NOMENCLATURE OF
A WATCHBAND

Memorize the various parts of the watchband listed below before you begin this project. Reference to these watchband parts are used throughout the instructions.

WATCHBAND BASE the portion of the watchband that fits around the wrist or arm, connecting to a commercial watch at one end and a commercial watchband spring bar at the other end

RECTANGULAR CUT OUT the cutout section at the one end of the watchband base that connects to the commercial watchband spring bar

SPRING PIN TUBE the round hollow tube at one end of the watchband base that encases a commercial spring pin which in turn connects to the watch spring pin holes

BEZEL the part of the watchband that encircles the cabochon

CABOCHON the stone that fits inside the bezel

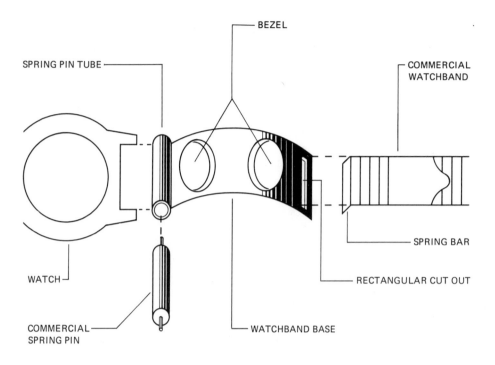

BEZEL

SPRING PIN TUBE

COMMERCIAL
WATCHBAND

COMMERCIAL
WATCHBAND

SPRING BAR

WATCH

RECTANGULAR CUT OUT

COMMERCIAL
SPRING PIN

WATCHBAND BASE

Figure XII–1 Nomenclature of a watchband

The purpose of this project is to introduce the beginning silversmith to the art of complex sawing, filing, and finishing. A man's watchband was chosen to illustrate these tasks, and also for the practical use that the silversmith may put it to—of wearing and displaying his work publicly.

It is also important to remember that a woman's watchband is accomplished in the same way, but on a smaller scale. When you have finished this project and wear it in public, prepare yourself for many compliments from your friends and relatives. Follow each step closely. Good luck!

STEP 1. For this project you will need the following supplies: one piece of 1 inch × 3 inches of 20-gauge S/S sheet, 1½ inches of 12-gauge S/S round tubing, 8 inches of 26-gauge × ⅛-inch S/S plain bezel, two 12mm × 10mm cabochons of your choice, and two 14mm × 10mm cabochons of your choice. (NOTE: I am using four free-form Spectrolite cabochons which are approxi-

93

mately the same size as the cabochons listed above. If you desire to use free-form cabochons instead of standard cabochons, make sure that the stones are not larger than the width and length of the watchband.) Additional commercial supplies will be needed to complete this project. These include a watch of your choice, two commercial spring pins, and a commercial watchstrap with a clasp and removable links (so that you will be able to adjust it to the proper size.) A three-link watchband is usually available from your supplier.

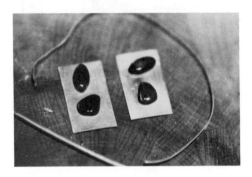

Figure XII–2 Supplies

STEP 2.   Utilizing the commercial watch for which you are creating the watchband, place the 20-gauge sheet next to the watch as shown in the photograph. Measure and mark with a pencil the distance between the spring pin holes of the watch on the 20-gauge silver sheet. Although the distance of the pin spring holes on a watch are of standard size, it is wise to custom measure this distance. Measure the distance between the two spring pin hole marks and cut the 20-gauge silver sheet using this measurement as the width and 1½ inches as the length. Repeat the above process by duplicating another watchband base. My two watchband bases measure $^{13}/_{16}$ inch × 1½ inches.

Figure XII–3 Marking with the watch on silver sheet with pencil

STEP 3.   A rectangular cutout must be made at the end of each watchband base in order to attach a spring bar from a commercial watchband. The rectangular cut should be approximately $1/16$ inch $\times$ $9/16$ inch. Use the spring bar of the commercial watchband which you intend to use as a guide in determining the width of the rectangular cutout. Mark the distance with a pencil as shown.

Figure XII–4   Marking with the watchband on silver sheet

STEP 4.   With a pencil, connect the two pencil marks made in the last step with a straight line $1/16$ inch in from the end of the watchband base. Draw another line parallel to the first line, $1/16$ inch from the first line. Connect the two parallel lines. Pencil in the rectangular cutout drawing as shown.

Figure XII–5   Using pencil on cutout

STEP 5.   Place the watchband base on a hard surface with the drawing of the rectangular cutout facing upward. With a center punch, tap an indentation directly in the middle of the rectangular cutout drawing as shown.

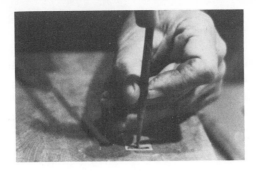

Figure XII–6 Using center punch on cutout

STEP 6. Place the watchband base in a vise. Using a hand drill with a drill bit, size less than $1/16$ inch in diameter, drill a small hole through the silver sheet at the point at which you made the indentation with the center punch in the previous step.

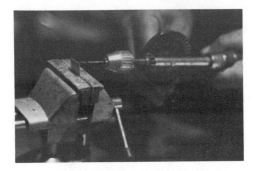

Figure XII–7 Drilling hole in cutout

STEP 7. Using a jeweler's saw with a size 3/9, 4/0, or 5/0 saw blade, insert one end of the saw blade through the drilled hole and attach it to the saw frame. Make sure that the saw blade is taut or it may break. With slow and deliberate strokes, cut out the drawn rectangular shape, closely following the penciled lines that you have drawn.

Figure XII–8 Using saw on cutout

STEP 8.   After you have completed cutting out the rectangular section on the watchband base, file off all sections that are uneven and rough, using a flat needle file. When you are finished, your two watchband bases should be similar to those in the photograph shown.

Figure XII–9   Cutouts

STEP 9.   On the other end of the watch strap base it is necessary to attach a spring pin tube which is used to hold a spring pin that attaches directly to a watch. To do this step you must use tubing that is large enough to allow a spring pin to be inserted inside the tube. Twelve-gauge tubing should be sufficient to receive a spring pin. With the 12-gauge tubing, measure the distance between the spring pin holes of the watch as shown. Mark the tubing with a pencil. Reduce this measurement by ⅛ inch and cut the tubing with a jeweler's saw. The ⅛ inch reduction will allow a free movement or space to accommodate the insertion of the spring pin into the spring pin holes of the watch at a later time. File the ends lightly with a flat needle file to make sure they are smooth and even.

Figure XII–10   Marking tubing wire with width of watch

STEP 10.   Place the watchband base on the soldering block. Place the spring pin tubing against the end of the watchband base and center as shown. Make sure that the spacing is equal on both ends of the watchband base. Clean the parts to be soldered with light steel wool. Apply silver soldering flux to the seam created by the tubing and the watchband base end. Place a medium-sized piece of HARD Silver Solder on the seam.

Figure XII–11   Placing solder on tubing and sheet seam

STEP 11.   Caution must be used in soldering the spring pin tube to the watchband base. The spring pin tube is hollow, and due to this structure it has a tendency to heat up to the melting point much faster than the watchband base. To reduce this possibility, apply a medium flame from your propane torch to the watchband base first, moving it in a circular motion, then move closer to the spring pin tubing as the heating of the metal reaches the solder's melting point. When this critical point is reached, apply the flame in short bursts to the seam between the spring pin tubing and the watchband base until the solder melts and runs into the seam. As soon as you observe this happening, PULL THE FLAME AWAY QUICKLY or you may melt the spring pin tubing. Cool in water. Repeat the above instructions for the other watchband base.

STEP 12.   After you have completed the steps above, your two watchband bases should look similar to those in the photograph shown.

Figure XII–12 Tubing soldered to silver sheet

STEP 13. Place the four cabochons in position on the watchband base and position them to your satisfaction. Check to make sure that the stones are not too big for the watchband bases.

Figure XII–13 Placing cabochon on watchband base

STEP 14. Utilizing all the knowledge you have acquired in Projects 1, 2, and 3, enclose the four cabochons with bezels and place them on the watchband bases as shown to determine the positioning you desire. Solder all the bezel seams with HARD Silver Solder and cool in water. (NOTE: If you are using free-form cabochons, the procedure for making the bezels is the same as for the standard sized cabochons, except that is takes a little more effort to surround the oddly shaped cabochons.

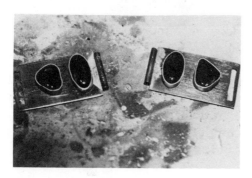

Figure XII–14 Surrounding cabochons with bezels

STEP 15.   Reform the bezels to the cabochons and clean the bottoms of the bezels by rubbing them on emery cloth. Place the bezels on the cleaned watchband base and position them as you desire. Do not have the bezels located closer than 1/8 inch from each other. Spacing of the cabochons should be even. (IMPORTANT NOTE: Face the soldered bezel seams toward the rectangular cutout and not toward the spring pin tube. Bezel seams can become ugly and are better off facing away from the watch.) Apply silver soldering flux to all bezels and bezel bases. Place two pieces of MEDIUM Silver Solder inside each bezel as you did in Project 1.

STEP 16.   Apply a heavy flame from your propane torch to one watchband base at a time, heating the whole project and moving it in a circular motion until the solder melts and runs completely around each bezel. Place the project in water for cooling. Repeat the same steps on the other watchband base. Both of your watchband bases should now be similar to those in the photograph below. Place the projects in pickling solution until all the fire scale is removed, then rinse with water.

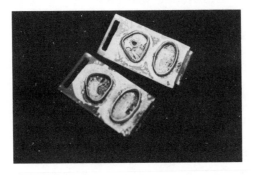

Figure XII–15   Soldered bezels to bezel bases

STEP 17.   Using your bracelet mandrel, place the watchband base on the mandrel as shown and press downward on both ends to form a curved contour that will adapt to your arm or wrist. The amount of the curved contour should be no more than is needed to ensure a proper fit for the arm or wrist.

Figure XII–16 Forming watchband base to bracelet mandrel

STEP 18. By forming the curved contour as detailed in the last step you will note that the bezels have become misaligned. With a curved burnisher, realign the bezels, working from the inside of the bezel and forcing the bezel outward at the points where needed.

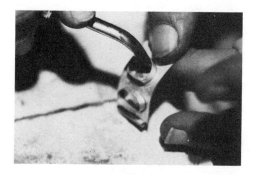

Figure XII–17 Using burnisher to straighten bezels

STEP 19. After realigning the bezels as detailed in the last step, the cabochons should fit easily into the bezels as shown.

Figure XII–18 Placing cabochon inside bezel

STEP 20.   You will also note that the watchband base, inside the bezel, is not perfectly flat due to the curved contours. To correct this problem, and to provide a flat bed for the cabochon to sit in, place a little sawdust inside the bezel to create a soft flat bed as shown. Place the cabochon inside the bezel to test for height. If the cabochon sits too high or too low, add or remove an amount of sawdust as needed.

Figure XII–19   Placing sawdust inside bezel

STEP 21.   Compress the bezel around the cabochons by using a curved burnisher as you learned in Project 1.

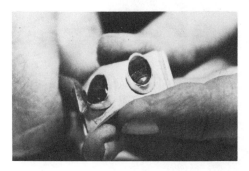

Figure XII–20   Using burnisher to close bezel around cabochon

STEP 22.   A difficult section of the watchband to finish correctly is the outside seam between the bezel and the watchband base. The seam is quite visible and must be removed to give the watchband a professional finished appearance. This can be accomplished by using a felt crevice buff with a tapered edge and tripoli compound. Be sure that the point of the tapered edge reaches into the seam as shown.

Figure XII–21 Using tapered buff on bezel seams

STEP 23. Another difficult section of the watchband to finish is the seam between the watchband base and the spring pin tube where the seam is quite visible and a buildup of silver solder exists. This can be removed by using a felt crevice buff with a tapered edge and tripoli compound. Run the sharp edge of the buff back and forth over the seam until the seam and excess solder are removed. Be especially careful not to wear through the spring pin tubing with the tripoli compound. Remember that tripoli compound is a very strong abrasive and removes surface metal at a very rapid rate. Note the position of the tapered buff in the photograph as shown.

Figure XII–22 Using tapered buff on tubing and sheet seam

STEP 24. Follow the finishing steps you learned in the previous projects, completing the final polishing with jeweler's red rouge compound.

STEP 25. Obtain two commercial spring pins to attach the watchband base to the watch. Also obtain a commercial watchband with clasp to attach to the other end of the watchband base. Make sure that the commercial watchband has removable links which you can shorten to fit your wrist or arm.

STEP 26. A picture of the finished man's watchbands.

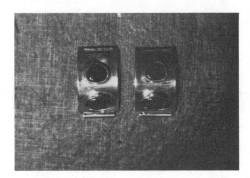

Figure XII–23

STEP 27. A picture of the finished watchband attached to a commercial watch.

Figure XII–24

XIII
MAKING A MAN'S BELT BUCKLE
Project 5

NOMENCLATURE OF A BELT BUCKLE

Memorize the various parts of the belt buckle listed below before you begin this project. Reference to these belt buckle parts is used throughout the instructions.

TOP BELT BUCKLE PLATE the front or face of the belt buckle

BOTTOM BELT BUCKLE PLATE the section that is soldered to the back portion of the top belt buckle plate

BELT BUCKLE LOOP the rectangular wire secured to the hinges on the back of the belt buckle and used to secure or anchor one end of a leather belt

HINGES the two curved half-round wires that secure the belt buckle loop to the back of the belt buckle

TONGUE the small tooth shaped projection that is soldered to the back of the belt buckle and utilized to fit into the holes in a leather belt, securing it to the belt buckle

Figure XIII–1 Nomenclature of a belt buckle

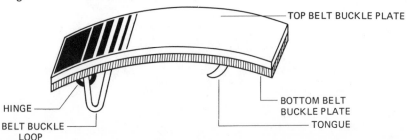

The purpose of this project is to give the beginning silver-smith the experience of creating a cutout overlay, in which a designed cutout sheet of sterling silver is soldered to the top of an equally sized sheet of sterling silver to obtain an etched effect. It will also give the beginner an opportunity to experience his first project with a movable part.

A three inch by two inch belt buckle was chosen because of the popularity of that size. This belt buckle is fashioned for a belt width of 1½ inches. As belt sizes change to meet fashion-able styles, the size of the belt buckle project can increase or decrease to meet the changing fashions. You will note that this project is totally handcrafted without the use of cabochons. Good luck!

STEP 1.   You will need the following supplies to complete this project: 3 inch × 2 inch of 20-gauge S/S sheet, 3¼ inch × 2¼ inch of 24-gauge S/S sheet, ¼-inch piece of 8-gauge S/S square wire, 1 inch of 8-gauge S/S half-round wire, and 6 inches of 10-gauge S/S round wire.

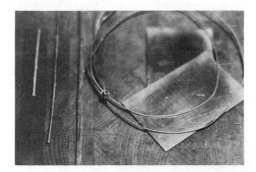

Figure XIII–2 Supplies

STEP 2.   Using a letter stencil sheet of your choice, center the stencil and outline your initials on the surface of the 3 inch × 2 inch 20-gauge silver sheet. Use an extra sharp pencil when outlining the letters to reduce shrinking of letter size. (NOTE: If you are talented in printing letters, you can print your initials freehand, without the use of a stencil.)

Figure XIII–3 Using a pencil with stencil

STEP 3. Using a center punch, make an indentation on the silver sheet on the section where your initials are to be cut out. Make sure that the indentation is at the widest part of each initial and centered perfectly between the drawn lines. These indentations will act as a drilling point on the next step.

Figure XIII–4 Using a center punch on lettering

STEP 4. Secure the initialed silver sheet in a vise. Using a hand drill with a drill bit size smaller than the width of the initials drawn, drill a hole at each indentation made in the previous step.

Figure XIII–5 Drilling hole in letters

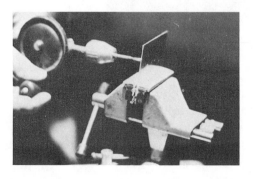

STEP 5.   Using a jeweler's saw with a size 3/0, 4/0, or 5/0 saw blade, disconnect one end of the saw blade and insert it through the first drilled hole, connecting it back up to the saw frame. Make sure that the saw blade is taut. Slowly and carefully, with deliberate strokes, cut out the first initial, closely following the lines you have drawn. Repeat the same process in cutting out the rest of your initials.

Figure XIII–6   Sawing out letters

STEP 6.   With a flat and a half-round needle file, smooth out and even all the edges on the initial cutouts as shown.

Figure XIII–7   Filing letters

STEP 7.   Clean both the 3 inch × 2 inch and 3¼ inch × 2¼ inch sterling silver sheets with light steel wool as shown. Make sure that all the impurities are removed. Be sure that both silver sheets are perfectly flat by using a rawhide mallet on a flat surface.

Figure XIII–8 Using steel wool on two silver sheets

STEP 8. Place the 3¼ inch × 2¼ inch silver sheet on a soldering block and apply silver soldering flux to the entire surface. Place the initialed 3 inch × 2 inch silver sheet on top of the 3¼ inch × 2¼ inch sheet, allowing a ¼ inch lip to extend out on all sides. This lip allows for the placement of large pieces of solder. Place enough HARD Silver Solder around the bottom lip of the 20-gauge silver sheet to cover fifty percent of the lip surface. You cannot use too much solder on this step.

Figure XIII–9 Placing solder on top and bottom sheets

STEP 9. Apply a heavy flame from the propane torch to the entire project, working your flame in a circular motion from the center of the belt buckle outward to the ends. This technique will cause the HARD Silver Solder to flow inward from the end toward the center of the project, thus sealing all points between the top and bottom sheets. When the belt buckle turns cherry red in color, PULL YOUR FLAME AWAY. Cool the project in water. Check to see if the silver solder has sealed the two plates together on all edges. If there are places between the two plates that did not seal, apply flux and MEDIUM Silver Solder to these areas and repeat the above soldering steps until all edges are completely soldered.

STEP 10.   Trim away the extra ¼-inch lip on the belt buckle with your metal shears and file the edges to a smooth and even finish with a regular flat file. Be sure to file deep enough to remove the soldered seam, which is quite visible, between the top and bottom silver plates.

STEP 11.   To curve the contour of your belt buckle slightly, place the belt buckle on the largest portion of the bracelet mandrel and push down with your hands on the outside edges as shown. (NOTE: This step is not necessary if you wish to maintain a flat contour.)

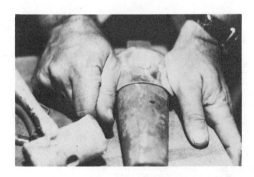

Figure XIII–10 Forming belt buckle to mandrel shape

STEP 12.   In creating hinges for the belt buckle loop which anchors the leather belt, use a pair of round-nosed pliers to bend a small end section of the 8-gauge half-round wire as shown.

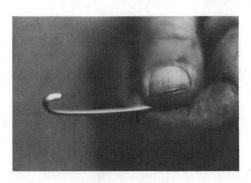

Figure XIII–11 Bent wire to be used as hinges

STEP 13.   Use a jeweler's saw to cut off the curved hinges, making sure that both open ends are even as shown.

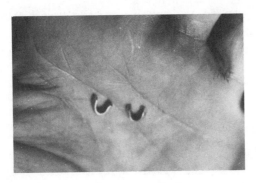

Figure XIII–12   Two hinges

STEP 14.   It is important that the curve of the hinges be large enough to accommodate the 10-gauge round wire as shown. Make sure that the 10-gauge round wire has sufficient room to move in all directions.

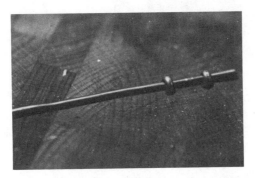

Figure XIII–13   Two hinges with round wire

STEP 15.   In creating the belt buckle loop, measure one inch in from the end of the 10-gauge round wire and mark with a pencil. Measure 1¾ inches in from the same end of the round wire and mark with a pencil. Again, measure 3½ inches in from the end and place a mark. Then, measure 4¼ inches in from the end and mark. And last, measure 5½ inches in from the end and mark. Cut the round wire at this point. Using flat-nosed pliers bend the 10-gauge round wire at the 1¾ inch mark as shown.

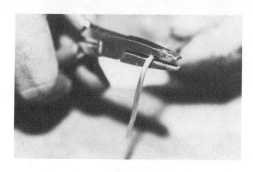

Figure XIII–14 Bending round wire with flat-nosed pliers

STEP 16. Bend the 10-gauge round wire at the 3½ inch mark, keeping the bent portions parallel with each other as shown. Check to be sure that the distance between the bent sections is not wider than the width of the belt buckle and yet wide enough to accommodate the leather belt you intend to use. If the fit is not satisfactory, readjust your measurements and repeat the above steps.

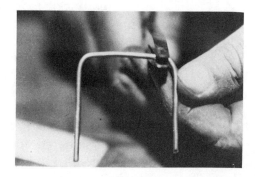

Figure XIII–15 Bending wire with flat-nosed pliers

STEP 17. Complete bending the belt buckle loop at the measured points until it appears similar to that in the photograph shown. (NOTE: The wire may overlap at the ends. If so, cut the wires off with a jeweler's saw, allowing about a ¹/₁₆-inch to ¼-inch gap as shown.

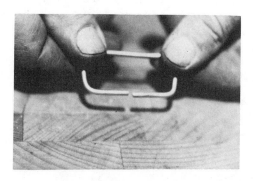

Figure XIII–16 Completed belt buckle loop

STEP 18.   Test your belt buckle loop with the hinges, as shown. Be sure that there is plenty of room for movement of the belt buckle loop.

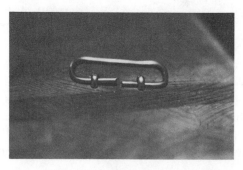

Figure XIII–17   Belt buckle loop and hinges

STEP 19.   Place the belt buckle loop on the back portion of the belt buckle plate as shown. Make sure that the belt buckle loop is located on the back of the belt buckle and opposite your last initial, because leather belts fasten to the belt buckle from the left, not the right, side. Place the hinges about ⅜ inch from the edges as shown and around the 10-gauge belt buckle loop as shown. It is important to have the hinges placed as close to the bend in the belt buckle loop as possible in order to restrict any excess lateral movement, although slight lateral movement is necessary. After having made sure that all parts to be soldered are clean, apply silver soldering flux to the end portions of the hinges only and where they touch the back of the belt buckle. Using a small soft artist's brush dipped in silver soldering flux, apply a small dot of MEDIUM Silver Solder to all four seams where the hinge ends rest upon the belt buckle. With the solder in place, make sure that the belt buckle loop is free and not touching any portion of the hinges. Remember that you are not soldering the belt buckle loop to the hinges or the back of the belt buckle. The belt buckle loop must be free to move after the hinges are soldered.

Figure XIII–18   Placing solder on hinges

STEP 20.   Use a heavy flame from your propane torch and apply the flame to one hinge at a time. Move in a circular motion. As soon as the solder melts and flows under the hinge, PULL THE FLAME AWAY IMMEDIATELY. If you wait too long the solder may flow under the belt buckle loop and solder it to the back of the belt buckle. When you have completed soldering the hinges, cool in water.

STEP 21.   The belt buckle loop should now be free and movable, yet secured to the back of the belt buckle by two hinges as shown.

Figure XIII–19   Belt buckle loop after soldering hinges

STEP 22.   In creating a stationary tongue which is to be secured to the back of the belt buckle, stand a ¼-inch 8-gauge square wire on its flat end, approximately ¼ inch in from the end of the belt buckle and centered in the middle as shown.

Figure XIII–20   Stationary tongue

STEP 23.   Clean the bottom of the 8-gauge square wire and the back portion of the belt buckle with light steel wool. Apply silver soldering flux to the seam to be soldered. Place a medium-sized piece of EASY Silver Solder to the seam between the bottom end of the square wire where it meets the belt buckle.

STEP 24.   Using a medium flame from your propane torch, apply the flame to the seam, moving it in a circular motion, until the solder melts and flows under the square wire.

STEP 25.   Use a half-round needle file to shape the tongue into a curved tooth shape as shown.

Figure XIII–21   Tooth-shaped tongue

STEP 26.   Place the project in a pickling solution for about thirty minutes or until all the fire scale is removed and the project turns a pure white color. Remove from the pickling solution, rinse in water, and dry.

STEP 27.   Finish your project, following the steps you learned in Project 1, using tripoli and red rouge compounds. (NOTE: You will notice that the belt buckle will have a very high shiny luster, almost too much for the size of this project. To soften this high luster, rub the project with medium steel wool, making sure that you rub from left to right only. This will give your belt buckle a more subdued and attractive finish.)

STEP 28.   To make your initials stand out and become more prominent, use an oxidizing solution which you can purchase from your supplier. Apply the oxidation solution with a small soft artist's paintbrush, as shown. Allow the oxidizing solution to turn the silver initials black. Wait thirty seconds and wash the oxidation off with clear water. After drying, brush lightly over the surface of the belt buckle with a medium steel wool to remove any excess oxidation around the edge of the initials.

Figure XIII–22 Applying oxidizing solution to letters

STEP 29. A view of the back of the finished belt buckle.

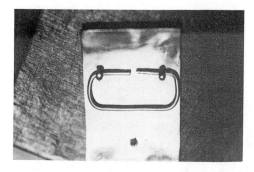

Figure XIII–23 Back of a finished belt buckle

STEP 30. A view of the front of the finished belt buckle.

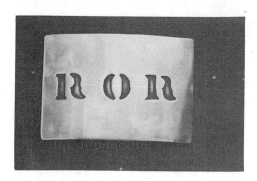

Figure XIII–24 Front view of a finished belt buckle

STEP 31. Attach the belt buckle to your leather belt as shown.

Figure XIII–25 Belt buckle attached to a leather belt

117

XIV
MAKING
A WOMAN'S
PENDANT
Project 6

NOMENCLATURE OF A PENDANT

Memorize the various parts of the pendant listed below before you begin this project. Reference to these pendant parts is used throughout the instructions.

PENDANT RING the outside oval edge that makes up the shape of the pendant

PENDANT STRUT the eight strips of flat wire that connect the cabochon base to the pendant ring

CABOCHON BASE the platform that supports the cabochon

PRONGS the four small round wires that secure the cabochon to the cabochon base

PENDANT EYELET the ring at the top of the pendant that attaches to the chain or jump ring

CABOCHON the stone that rests on the cabochon base and is held down by prongs

Figure XIV–1 Nomenclature of a woman's pendant

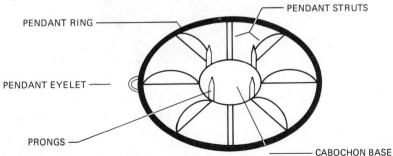

The object of this project is to introduce the beginning silversmith to a more complicated process of creating jewelry. This delicate creation will probably prove to be the most challenging project in this series. Good luck!

STEP 1.   You will need the following supplies to complete this project: five inches of ⅛ inch × 18-gauge S/S flat wire, one piece of 1 inch × ¾ inch of 26-gauge S/S sheet, two inches of 18-gauge S/S half-round wire, ½ inch of 16-gauge S/S half-round wire, and one 13mm × 18mm cabochon of your choice. I will use a Botswana cabochon for this project.

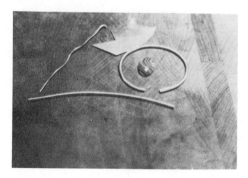

Figure XIV–2 Supplies

STEP 2.   Using a cobochon template and a very sharp pencil, draw the outline shape of a 13mm × 18mm cabochon on the 26-gauge sterling silver sheet as shown.

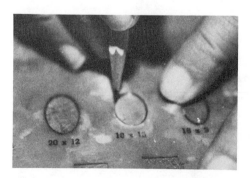

Figure XIV–3 Using pencil and template to outline on silver sheet

STEP 3.   Fit your 13mm × 18mm cabochon over the outline you drew in Step 2 in order to make sure of the correct size.

Figure XIV–4 Placing cabochon on silver sheet

STEP 4. Cut out the cabochon base along the lines that you have drawn in the previous step. Recheck the size of the cabochon and the cutout cabochon base again to see if they are exactly the same size.

Figure XIV–5 Cabochon and cabochon base

STEP 5. Use a flat needle file to smooth and even the outside edge of the cabochon base as shown.

Figure XIV–6 Filing cabochon base

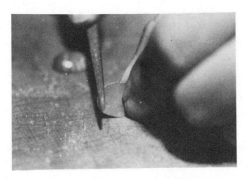

STEP 6.   Place 5½ inches of 10-gauge round wire around the bracelet mandrel and form the wire into an oval shape. Utilize the rawhide mallet to help you achieve the proper oval shape.

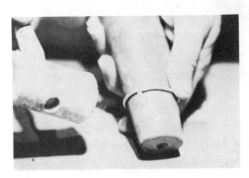

Figure XIV–7   Forcing round wire around bracelet mandrel with rawhide mallet

STEP 7.   Overlap the ends of the 10-gauge round wire as shown. Place the pendant ring in a vise and cut through both overlapped wires with a jeweler's saw so that both ends have identical shapes. Butt both ends together and place on a soldering block.

Figure XIV–8   Oval round wire, showing overlap

STEP 8.   Apply silver soldering flux to the seam and place a small piece of HARD Silver Solder on the seam.

STEP 9.   Apply a heavy flame from your propane torch in a back and forth motion over the seam until the solder melts and flows into the seam. Cool in water.

STEP 10.   Place the soldered pendant ring on a charcoal block and place soldering pins on the inside to secure the ring to the charcoal block as shown. This will keep the pendant ring from moving.

Figure XIV–9 Pendant ring secured to charcoal block with soldering pins

STEP 11. Place the cabochon base directly in the center of the pendant ring, using a ruler to check the distance from the cabochon base edge to the outside portion of the pendant ring as shown.

Figure XIV–10 Centering cabochon base inside pendant ring with ruler

STEP 12. Your cabochon base should be perfectly centered in the middle of the pendant ring and appear similar to that in the photograph shown. The cabochon base will now be connected to the pendant ring by pendant struts as detailed in the next few steps.

Figure XIV–11 Cabochon base centered inside pendant ring

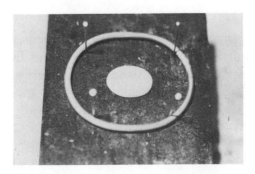

STEP 13. To create a pendant strut, measure the distance between the edge of the cabochon base to the inside portion of the pendant ring. When you obtain an exact measurement, add $1/16$ inch to the length and cut to size. With a jeweler's saw, cut a $1/16$ inch × $1/16$ inch notch in one corner of the strut as shown.

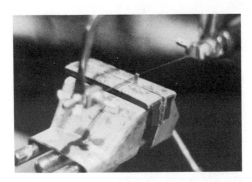

Figure XIV–12 Sawing out notch on pendant strut

STEP 14. Your pendant strut with the cut out notch should look similar to the photograph shown. The notched portion of the pendant strut will act as a platform for the cabochon base to rest upon.

Figure XIV–13 Notched out pendant strut

STEP 15. Use soldering pins to support the strut as shown. Be sure that the notch cut out is at the top of the strut and in the center of the pendant ring. The opposite end should be butted up against the pendant ring where the soldering will take place. Your soldering pins should not be near this soldering seam or they may be soldered to the project.

Figure XIV–14 Securing pendant strut to pendant ring by soldering pins

STEP 16. With the soldering joint clean, apply a drop of silver soldering flux where the pendant strut butts up against the pendant ring. Place a small piece of MEDIUM Silver Solder on the seam.

STEP 17. Apply a medium flame from your torch, rotating it in a circular motion around the seam until the solder melts and flows into the seam. Cool in water. (NOTE: As you are soldering the struts to the outside pendant ring, the heat from your torch may cause the pendant ring to expand and pull away from the strut. In this case, simply use a pair of tweezers while still applying heat and move the pendant ring in both toward and against the pendant strut.)

STEP 18. Solder the second opposite strut as shown, using the same method as described above.

Figure XIV–15 Securing two pendant struts to pendant ring by soldering pins

STEP 19. Solder the third strut as shown.

Figure XIV–16 Securing the third pendant strut to pendant ring by soldering pins

STEP 20. Solder the fourth strut as shown.

Figure XIV–17 Securing the fourth pendant strut to pendant ring by soldering pins

STEP 21. Using a flat needle file, smooth out and even the notches on the four struts as shown so that the cabochon base will sit firmly into the notches.

Figure XIV–18 Smoothing out notches with file

STEP 22. Place the cabochon base plate into the center of the pendant, making sure that it fits evenly into the notches as shown.

Figure XIV–19 Inserting cabochon base into notches of pendant struts

STEP 23. Apply silver soldering flux to all four joints to be soldered. Place a small piece of MEDIUM Silver Solder on the seams between the cabochon base and the notches of the struts.

Figure XIV–20 Placing solder on cabochon base and pendant struts

STEP 24. Apply a medium flame from your propane torch to each seam, one at a time, maintaining a small circular motion until the solder melts and flows into the seam. After you have finished all four seams, cool in water.

STEP 25. With the cabochon base firmly soldered in place, your project should now look similar to the photograph shown.

Figure XIV–21 Cabochon base soldered to all four pendant struts

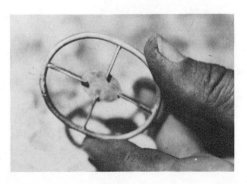

STEP 26. Measure and cut out the four remaining struts in the same manner as you did the first four struts and position them diagonally as shown.

Figure XIV–22 Positioning diagonal struts between cabochon base and pendant ring

STEP 27. Be sure that all points to be soldered have been cleaned with steel wool. Apply silver soldering flux to each seam that contacts the cabochon base plate and the outside pendant ring.

STEP 28. Place a small piece of EASY Silver Solder to all eight seams that are to be soldered.

STEP 29. Using a medium flame from your propane torch, apply the flame in a circular motion to one seam at a time, moving onto the next seam as soon as the solder melts and flows into the seam. Cool the project in water.

STEP 30. The back of your project should now look similar to the photograph shown.

Figure XIV–23 Back portion of pendant

STEP 31. A flat needle file should be used to smooth off all the rough sections that were built up during the soldering. Round off the top section of the strut notch so that it shows a slight slope toward the cabochon base.

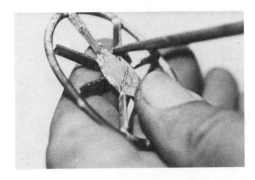

Figure XIV–24   Using needle file

STEP 32.   With a large flat file, smooth off the outside portion of the struts where they connect to the pendant ring. Continue to level off the struts with the pendant ring so that the soldering seam between the two is not visible.

Figure XIV–25   Using large file to smooth ends of struts

STEP 33.   The top of your project should now look similar to the photograph shown.

Figure XIV–26   Filed struts

STEP 34. Test to see that the cabochon now fits flat into the cabochon base as shown. Be sure that the pendant struts do not interfere with the cabochon. If the struts obstruct the setting of the cabochon, use a needle file to reduce the strut obstruction.

Figure XIV–27 Fitting cabochon onto cabochon base

STEP 35. Place the project on a charcoal block, face up, and place four ½-inch long pieces of 18-gauge half-round wire into the charcoal block next to and against the diagonal struts and cabochon base as shown. The wire should be pushed deeply enough into the charcoal block to allow ¼ inch of wire to be above the cabochon base. The 18-gauge half-round wire will be used at a later time as prongs to hold the cabochon firmly in place.

Figure XIV–28 Placing prongs next to cabochon base and into charcoal block

STEP 36. Apply silver soldering flux to the seams where the half-round wire touches the struts and the cabochon base. Using a small artist's brush dipped in silver soldering flux, place a small piece of EASY Silver Solder to each seam.

Figure XIV–29 Placing solder on prongs and cabochon base

STEP 37. Apply a low flame from your propane torch to the cabochon base plate, using a circular motion, until the solder melts and flows into the seams of the half-round wire, cabochon base, and the pendant struts. Cool in water.

STEP 38. Working from the back of the pendant, cut off the excess half-round wire that was inserted into the charcoal in the previous step.

Figure XIV–30 Trimming prongs

STEP 39. Use your needle files to remove any excess round wire that will not be part of the prong stems. Round off the top of each of the four prongs so that they will fit smoothly against the cabochon. All prongs should be ¼ inch above the cabochon base.

Figure XIV–31 Filing prongs

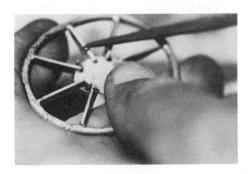

STEP 40.   To make a pendant eyelet for connecting a chain or jump ring, use a ½ inch piece of 16-gauge half-round wire. Using round-nosed pliers, curl the half-round wire into a half-circle and place it at the top of the project as shown. The flat side of the half-round wire should be on the inside of the half-circle.

Figure XIV–32   Pendant eyelet attached to pendant ring

STEP 41.   Apply silver soldering flux to the two seams that connect the pendant eyelet and the pendant ring. Place a small piece of EASY Silver Solder on each seam.

STEP 42.   Use a medium flame from your propane torch, moving it in a small circular motion above the eyelet, until the solder melts and flows into the seams. Cool in water.

STEP 43.   File all rough edges of the eyelet smooth and place the project in a pickling solution for about thirty minutes or until all the fire scale is removed and the project turns a pure white color. Remove the project from the pickling solution, rinse with water, and dry.

STEP 44.   Place the cabochon on the cabochon base plate. With the curved burnisher, push the prongs gently but firmly inward and downward against the cabochon until the cabochon is held firmly by the four prongs.

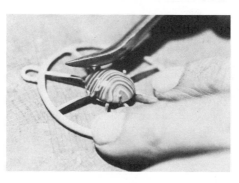

Figure XIV–33   Forcing prongs against cabochon with burnisher

STEP 45.   Following the finishing procedures you learned in Project 1, polish off the project, using tripoli and jeweler's red rouge compound.

STEP 46.   For a more professional effect, apply oxidizing solution to the inside of the struts. Apply the oxidizing solution with an artist's brush as shown. Wait thirty seconds and rinse the project with water. Dry the project and rebuff the areas where excess oxidation has taken place.

Figure XIV–34 Oxidizing inside portion of pendant struts

STEP 47.   A back view of the finished woman's pendant.

Figure XIV–35

STEP 48.   A front view of the finished woman's pendant.

Figure XIV–36

STEP 49.   A side view of the finished woman's pendant.

Figure XIV–37

STEP 50.   A finished view of the pendant attached to a jump ring and chain.

Figure XIV–38

GLOSSARY

ABRASIVE a compound that removes or roughens metal when applied with a buffing wheel

BELT BUCKLE LOOP a portion of a belt buckle that anchors one end of a belt

BEZEL a thin flat piece of metal that surrounds and holds a gem stone

BEZEL BASE the platform that supports a bezel

BEZEL TRIM a shaped wire that surrounds the soldered section between the bezel and the bezel base

BLEED the melting and flowing out of solder from a previously soldered seam

BOTTOM BELT BUCKLE PLATE the piece of sheet metal that is soldered to the bottom side of the top belt buckle plate

BRACELET HEAD the top portion of a bracelet which includes the bracelet base, bracelet bezel, and bracelet bezel trim

BRACELET MANDREL a solid tapered metal form that is used to shape metal, usually a bracelet

BRACELET SHANK the section of a bracelet that surrounds the wrist or arm

BRUSH WHEEL BUFF a polishing wheel with stiff bristles

BURNISHER a tool that is used to smooth out metal

BURRS a rough or jagged edge on metal

BUTT END a point at which a piece of metal comes to an end

CABOCHON a gem stone that is flat on the bottom and has a domed-shaped top

CENTER PUNCH a tool that comes to a point on one end and is used to indent metal

CHARCOAL BLOCK a soldering block made of charcoal

COMMERCIAL SPRING PIN metal tubing with two internal springs and two pins used to attach a watchband to a watch

COMMERCIAL SUPPLIES any supplies that are obtained from a retail or wholesale outlet

COMMERCIAL WATCH a watch that is obtained from a retail or wholesale outlet

COMMERCIAL WATCHBAND any watchband that is obtained from a retail or wholesale outlet

CONTOUR a surface line

COTTON BUFF a polishing wheel made' of cotton

CRAFTSMAN a person or artist who has mastered exceptional techniques in his craft

CRIMPING the bending or folding of metal

CURVED BURNISHER a curved tool used for smoothing metal

DIAMETER the distance across the middle of a circle

DOUBLE SHAFT MOTOR an electric motor that has a shaft extending outward from both sides

DRILL BIT a tool which is inserted into a drill to bore holes

EMERY CLOTH a piece of cloth coated with an abrasive called emery

ETCHED a design made on metal through the use of acid

EASY SOLDER a silver solder composed of 56 percent silver, with a melting point of 1145° Fahrenheit.

FELT CREVICE BUFF a felt polishing wheel with tapered edges

FIRE SCALE a buildup of impurities on metal resulting from extreme high temperatures

FLAT FILE a tool that is rectangular in shape with a flat rough surface used to remove metal

FLAT-NOSED PLIERS a pivoted tool with flat jaws, used in bending or holding metal

FLEXIBLE SHAFT MACHINE a hand-held drilling and polishing tool with an attached flexible shaft that connects to an electric motor

FLINT TORCH LIGHTER a tool that uses flint as a sparking element to ignite volatile gases

FLOWING POINT a specific point at which solder that is being heated melts and runs toward the highest temperature point

FLUX a chemical substance that aids solder in flowing on metal

FREE-FORM a particular shape that does not follow any particular geometric form

GAUGE a measurement of thickness

HALF-ROUND FILE a tool that is flat on one side and round on the other, with rough surfaces for removing metal

HAND DRILL a hand-held tool that turns a drill bit for the purpose of boring holes

HANDCRAFTED a crafted object skillfully constructed by hand rather than by machine

HANDMADE a crafted artpiece constructed entirely by hand, not by machine

HARD SOLDER a silver solder composed of 75 percent silver, with a melting point of 1365° Fahrenheit

HINGES curved metal that secures the belt buckle loop to the back of a belt buckle

JEWELER'S RED ROUGE a mild red colored abrasive for polishing metal

JEWELER'S SAW a framed tool with serrated blades for delicate cutting of fine metals

JEWELER'S SAW BLADE a blade that is used with a jeweler's saw to cut fine metal

JOINT the line between two pieces of metal that are to be soldered together

JUMP RING a round piece of metal that attaches a chain to a pendant

MEDIUM SOLDER a silver solder composed of 70 percent silver, with a melting point of 1275° Fahrenheit

METAL SHEARS a tool that cuts metal in scissor-like fashion

MELTING POINT an exact temperature at which various metals will change from a solid to a liquid

MILLIMETER a metric system measurement equal to 1 one-thousandth of a meter

NEEDLE FILE a small narrow file that is usually less than six inches long and, in most cases, is tapered on the end

NOMENCLATURE a term used to describe systematically different parts of an art object or scientific device

NOTCH a cut-out section of metal

OPTICAL VISOR a visual aid used for enlarging an object to be viewed

OVERBURN overheating a metal, causing it to reach its melting point

OVERLAY laying a designed cut-out sheet of metal directly on top of another sheet of metal

OXIDATION oxygen forming an oxide on metal

OXIDIZING SOLUTION a chemical that induces oxygen to combine with metal to form an oxide on metal

PENDANT EYELET a circular hole at the top of a pendant for attaching a chain or jump ring

PENDANT RING the metal ring that forms the outside shape of a pendant

PENDANT STRUT a metal piece that is used to form a connecting bridge between one section of a pendant to another

PICKLING SOLUTION an acid chemical solution that is used in removing oxides and fire scale from a metal

PLASTIC TONGS a plastic grasping tool with two arms that is used to remove objects from a solution

PLASTIC TRAY a shallow plastic container for holding various liquids

PRONGS tiny projections of metal that secure a gem stone in its setting

PROPANE TORCH a mechanical unit used to control the flow of ignited propane gas

RAWHIDE MALLET the head of a hammer that is constructed with layers of tightly bound leather and attached to a wooden handle

RIBBON SOLDER solder that is supplied in a ribbon form

RING BUFF a tapered flannel polishing unit that fits inside a ring shank

RING HEAD the top part of a ring which includes the bezel, bezel trim, and bezel base

RING MANDREL a tapered metal tool that is used to form the ring shank of a ring

ROUND-NOSED PLIERS a pivoted tool with round jaws used for bending metal into round forms

ROUND SOLDER solder that is supplied in round wire form

ROUND TUBING a cylindrically shaped metal that is hollow in the center

SAW FRAME a tool consisting of a handle and a frame, used for attaching a saw blade

SEAL the complete fusion of two pieces of metal together, using solder

SEAM the line between two pieces of metal that has been, or is about to be, soldered

SHEET SOLDER solder that is supplied in thin sheets

SILVERSMITH a person who makes and repairs objects made from silver

SILVER SOLDER an alloy primarily made from silver

SOLDERING BLOCK a fire-resistant platform for placing an object to be soldered upon

SOLDERING PINS heat-resistant straight pins used in supporting objects while they are being soldered

SPRING BAR the end piece of a metal watch strap that wraps around a spring pin

SPRING PIN HOLES the four holes in a commercial watch that receive the spring pin

SPRING PIN TUBE the hollow cylindrical part of a watchband that retains the spring pin

STENCIL a plastic, metal, or paper sheet with cut-out numbers and letters used to reproduce those numbers and letters on another object

STERLING SILVER a metal alloy composed of 92.5 percent silver and 7.5 percent copper

S/S a symbol for sterling silver

SUPPLIERS commercial sources where materials and supplies may be obtained

TAPERED BUFF a felt crevice polishing wheel with a tapered edge

TECHNIQUE a particular way of doing something

TEMPLATE a plastic, paper, or metal sheet with cut-out designs used to reproduce these designs on another subject

TONGUE the narrow stem of a belt buckle that secures one end of a leather belt by projecting it through the holes of the leather belt

TOP BELT BUCKLE PLATE the portion of the belt buckle that serves as the face or front of the belt buckle

VISE a metal clamping device used for holding objects

WATCHBAND BASE the part of a watchband that attaches to a watch at one end and to a spring bar at the other

SILVERSMITH SUPPLIER'S LIST

The following is a partial listing of two hundred and thirty suppliers located throughout the United States and Canada that service and supply the silversmith's needs. (Some of the listed suppliers offer free catalogs, while others do not.)

It would be best for the beginning silversmith to contact at least five of the suppliers listed so that prices and supplies may be compared.

I have not had personal dealings with most of the suppliers listed below; however, I have dealt with Allen's Rocks & Gifts; Baskin & Sons, Inc.; Bourget Brothers; California Crafts Supply; Fire Mountain Gems; Grieger's, Inc.; Kingsley North, Inc.; The Maisel Company; and The William Dixon Company. I have found them all to be extremely satisfactory and helpful.

Because of the diversity in the operations of various suppliers, it is impossible for this author or the publisher of this book to guarantee the performance, supplies, or services of any of the suppliers listed.

A & B Rock & Hobby Shop
218 North Main Street
Germantown, OH 45327

A & B Rock Shop
4518 Sandstone Drive
Williamson, MI 48895

A & G Rockfeller Lap
3121 West Burnham
Milwaukee, WI 53215

Ace Lapidary Supply, Inc.
6037 Sepulveda Blvd.
Van Nuys, CA 91411

Ace's Rock Shop
4112 Pennsylvania
Kansas City, MO 64111

Ackley's Rocks & Stamps
3230 North Stone Ave.
Colorado Springs, CO 80907

Adamas Lapidary & Gem, Inc.
8391 Market Street
Youngstown, OH 44512

Aka's Gems & Minerals
18113 Saticoy Street
Reseda, CA 91335

Alamosa Gems & Minerals
P.O. Box 1164
Alamosa, CO 81101

Alden Lapidary
57 Golf Drive
Painesville, OH 44077

Allen's Rocks & Gifts
27315 Detroit Road
Cleveland, OH 44145

Alpine Rock & Mineral Shop
20 West Evans Ave.
Denver, CO 80223

Anchor Tool & Supply Co., Inc.
P.O. Box 265
231 Main Street
Chatham, NJ 07928

Armadillo Farm General Store
    & Trading Company
Route 6—Box 55
Nacogdoches, TX 75962

Art Mart, Inc.
8112 Maryland Ave.
St. Louis, MO 63105

Art Parts Enterprise
P.O. Box 196
Cortaro, AZ 85230

Ascot Silver Mine
4214 Oak Lawn
Dallas, TX 75219

Ashley's Arts & Crafts
R.F.D. No. 1
Tonica, IL 61370

B & G Rock Shop
5th & Spruce
Dodge City, KS 67801

B & J Rock Shop
620 Claymont Estates Drive
Ballwin, MO 63011

B & T Rock Shop
1404 State Street
Bay City, MI 48706

Baber's Rock Shop
R.R. 2—Box 255 A
Ada, OH 45810

Bain's Rock Shop
1921 South Academy Dr.
Melbourne, FL 32901

Bakke Rock Shop
126–20th Street West
Saskatoon, Saskatchewan,
Canada S7M   0W6

Barnard's, Inc.
4724 Broadway
Kansas City, MO 64112

Baskin & Sons, Inc.
732 Union Avenue
Middlesex, NJ 08846

Bay Shore Rock Shop
3005 Memorial Drive
North Muskegon, MI 49445

Beckham's Barn
Route 2—Box 134
Irmo, SC 29063

Bellevue Rock Shop
2216 Lloyd Street
Bellevue, NB 68005

Bill's Rocks & Hobby
3458 South Acoma
Englewood, CO 80110

Bonnies Rock Shop
R.F.D. 2
Brigham, UT 84302

Bourget Brothers
1636 11th Street
Santa Monica, CA 90404

Bowser's
3317 State Street
Santa Barbara, CA 93105

C & R Enterprises
4833 East Park Street
Route 9—Box 545A
Springfield, MS 65804

California Crafts Supply
1096 North Main Street
Orange, CA 92667

California Lapidary Supply
321 N. Pacific Coast Highway
Redondo Beach, CA 90277

Cal-Tex Gems
1331 McHenry Ave.
Modesto, CA 95350

Canadian-American (Can-Am)
802 East Ave.
Erie, PA 16503

Capri Creations
1406 Sunset Blvd.
P.O. Box 8513
Waco, TX 76710

The Caprock
3700—14th Ave.
Rock Island, IL 61201

Carousel Gems & Minerals
132 South York Road
Hatboro, PA 19040

Charbonneau's Lapidary Service, Ltd.
4020 Bow Trail Southwest
Calgary, Alberta,
Canada T3C   3ML

Chipeta Gems
3325 U.S. Highway 24 West
Chipita Park, CO 80811

Cibola Gem & Mineral
1248 East Prince Road
Tucson, AZ 85719

Clark's Agate Shop
219 South 50th
Tacoma, WA 98408

Clevenger Hobby
8206 North Oak
Kansas City, MO 64118

Coffey's
9120 Jamacha Road
Spring Valley, CA 92077

Colorado Lapidary Supply
1900 East Lincoln
Fort Collins, CO 80521

Pat Cornish
P.O. Box 772
Brea, CA 92621

The Cotati Rock Shop
P.O. Box 237
Cotati, CA 94928

Country Mineral & Lapidary
Shop
R.D. 2
Elizabethtown Road
Ilion, NY 13357

The Craftsmen
221 Brighton Avenue
West End, NJ 07740

Crandall Lapidary, Inc.
G. L. 49 West Street
Annapolis, MD 21401

Cross Lapidary & Gem Shop
R. D. No. 2 China Hill Road
Box 180
Nassau, NY 12123

Crystal Cave
55 West Queen Street
Hampton, VA 23669

Crystal Mining Company, Inc.
188 Pollard Street
North Billerica, MA 01862

The Crystal Pocket, Inc.
23906 Lorain Road
North Olmsted, OH 44070

Crystal Rock Shop
166 McConnell Ave.
Elmira Heights, NY 14903

Danica Lapidary & Art Barn
Box 2471 (1215 Main Street)
Smithers, British Columbia,
Canada V0J   2N0

Daniels Lapidary & Jewelry
Parkway City Mall
Box 1563
Huntsville, AL 35801

Davis Crafts, Inc.
86 West Old Wilson Bridge Rd.
Columbus, OH 43085

The Dickey's
715 Lake Air Drive
Waco, TX 76710

Distinctive Jewelry
1419 B Street
Snyder, OK 73566

Dixie Gems & Minerals, Inc.
P.O. Box 7176
Montgomery, AL 36107

William Dixon Company
750 Washington Ave.
Carlstadt, NJ 07072

Doc's Rocks & Gifts
2690 28th Street
Boulder, CO 80301

Dondero's Rock & Mineral
Shop
Main Street
North Conway, NH 03860

Dublee Rocks & Gems
4731 South Columbus Place
Tulsa, OK 74105

Duck's Treasures
225 Lancaster Drive S. E.
Salem, OR 97301

Durrenberger Rock Shop
No. 1 Gaslight Square
Corpus Christi, TX 78404

East Coast Rock Exchange
14 Circle Drive
Mount Arlington, NJ 07856

Robert M. Eaton
54 Heberle Road
Rochester, NY 14609

Edmonton Rock & Gem Supply, Ltd.
6150-90 Avenue
Edmonton, Alberta,
Canada T6B   0P1

Ed's Gun & Rock Shop
308 West 3rd Street
P.O. Box 310
Desoto, KS 66018

The Elkins Gem Stones
833 South Main
P.O. Box 576
Prineville, OR 97754

Elmerk Service & Machine Co.
6545 East 11th Street
Tulsa, OK 74112

Evergreen Rockshop
Route 211, 3/4 mile East
New Market, VA 22844

Farmer's Gem Shop
10037 Cave Creek Road
Phoenix, AZ 85020

Fire Mountain Gems
11274 Ventura Blvd.
North Hollywood, CA 91604

Flounders Ornamental L.T.D.
2010 13th Ave.
North St. Petersburg, FL 33712

Donald L. Foltz
7401 North Layman Ave.
Indianapolis, IN 46250

Forsley's Rocks & Minerals
Oak Tree Corners Shopping
Center
430 Milwaukee Ave.
Lincolnshire, Prairie View
IL 60069

Fraziers Gems & Minerals
115 Center Street, Box 117
Seville, OH 44273

Frazier's Minerals & Lapidary
1724 University
Berkley, CA 94703

GP Rock Shop
110 South Jefferson Dr.
Huntington, WV 25701

G & G's Miracle House
5621 West Hemlock Street
Milwaukee, WI 53223

Gabriel Gem & Lapidary Supply
10725 Southeast Orient Drive
Boring, OR 97009

Gem Gallery
2100 Empire Blvd.
Rochester, NY 14580

The Gem Mine
495 Cedar Lane
Teaneck, NJ 07666

Gemcraft of Ohio
7510 Mentor Ave.
Mentor, OH 44060

Gems & Geodes
175 Post Road West
Westport, CT 06880

Gemstone Wonderland
4517–23rd Ave.
Moline, IL 61265

Geodes & Gems
55198 29 Palms Highway
Yucca Valley, CA 92284

Geophile Inc.
Route 434, Box 358
Apalachin, NY 13732

George's Craft Shop
5702 Harford Road
Baltimore, MD 21214

George's Lapidary
700 Portage Ave.
Winnipeg, Manitoba,
Canada R3G   0M6

The Getz's
168 Garland Ave.
Buffalo, NY 14206

Glendora Lapidary
130 North Glendora Ave.
Glendora, CA 91740

Goodnow Gems, U.S.A.
5740 Canyon Drive
Amarillo, TX 79109

Grants Pass Rock Shop & Museum
1495 Northeast 7th Street
Grants Pass, OR 97526

Gravois Rock Shop
Highway 5, Box 56
Gravois Mills, MO 56037

Grieger's, Inc.
Post Office Bin No. 41
Pasadena, CA 91109

Hall's of Denver
306 East Colfax
Denver, CO 80203

Hambaugh Bola Supply
2609 East Desert Cove
Phoenix, AZ 85028

Handley Rock Hobby
   Supplies, Inc.
6202 Hiway 99, Space No. 1
Vancouver, WA 98665

Harness Appliance
112 South Main
Elk City, OK 73644

Harter's Minerals
182 South Prospect St.
Spencerport, NY 14559

Heldon Rock Shop
223 Inverness Ave. East
Hamilton, Ontario,
Canada L9A   1H1

High Tide/Rock Bottom
1832 Coventry Road
Cleveland Heights, OH 44118

Hi Jolly Rockhound
P.O. Box 685
Quartsite, AZ 85346

Hutsell's Rock Shop
606 South 16th
Blue Springs, MO 64015

Indian Trading Post
828 Choctaw
Chickasha, OK 73018

International Gem Services
Suite No. 100
Executive Plaza Building
6501 Loisdale Court
Springfield, VA 22150

J & B Gems
4208 North Maine
Baldwin Park, CA 91706

J & J Rock Shop
Route 2, Box 696
Brazoria, TX 77422

Monroe D. Jacobs
5550 Indiana
Golden, CO 80401

Jeri's Rock Shop
14016 Wood Street
Harvey, IL 60426

The Jewelry Mart
P.O. Box 7447
Pueblo West, CO 81007

Jim's Gems (Inc.)
733 Route 23
Wayne, NJ 07470

Ken's Gems
33 State Road Route 7
Great Barrington, MA 01230

Ker-Ree Jewelry & Rock Shop
2124 North State Street
Belvidere, IL 61008

King's Gem Center
5510 North Freeway
Houston, TX 77076

Kingsley North, Inc.
910 Brown Street
Norway, MI 49870

Kohl's Rock Shop
928 Eubank Northeast
Albuquerque, NM 87112

Lapidary International
1228 South Beach Blvd.
Anaheim, CA 92804

Lapidary Supply Division of
    Colind Photography, Inc.
1327 Northeast Adams Street
Peoria, IL 61603

Lapidary Supply of Grand
Junction
1414 Colorado
Grand Junction, CO 81501

The Lapidary Workshop, Ltd.
3417 Greenville Ave.
Dallas, TX 75206

Latta's Gems & Minerals
2336 Broadway
Rockford, IL 61108

Lee's Jade and Opals, Ltd.
3563-232 Street   R.R. 3
Langley, British Columbia,
Canada V3A   4P6

Henry Les Lapidary
4102 Bussey Road
Syracuse, NY 13215

Lou-Bon Gems and Rocks
6349A Columbia Pike
Bailey's Crossroads, VA 22041

J. F. McAughin Company
2628 North River Ave.
Rosemead, CA 91770

M & W Crafts Studio
3202 Seymour Road
Eau Claire, WI 54701

Maine Mineral Jewelry
Cascade Road
Old Orchard, ME 04064

Maisel's Arts & Crafts
1500 Lomas Blvd. Northwest
Albuquerque, NM 87103

Manchester Minerals
13 Grovenor Street
Chester, Cheshire, England

Manchester Minerals
420 Manchester Road
Heaton Chapel
Stockport, Cheshire, England

Manchester Minerals
1 Tithebarn Street
Bury, Lancashire, England

Maral Rocks & Gems
558 Upper James Street
Hamilton, Ontario,
Canada L9C   2Y4

Mardis House of Gems &
Rocks
10370 North Intake (Highway
95)
Blythe, CA 92225

Marg Rock & Art Shop
P.O. Box 1315
8317 Wesley Street
Greenville, TX 75401

Martin's Rock Shop
817 Cook Ave.
Billings, MT 59101

Merry Artists Rock & Lapidary
Shop
1996 Kentucky Ave.
Winter Park, FL 32789

Metals 'N Tools, Ltd.
202 West Jericho Turnpike
Huntington Station, NY 11746

Michael's Lapidary
12282 Harbor Blvd.
Garden Grove, CA 92640

Michigan Lapidary Supply
Company
24735 Halstead Road
Farmington Hills, MI 48018

Mid-America Rock Shop
4503 North Milwaukee Ave.
Chicago, IL 60630

Mid Jersey Rock Shop
466-A New Brunswick Ave.
Fords, NJ 08863

Mid-West Lapidary, Inc.
17910 East 10 Mile Road
East Detroit, MI 48093

Miner's Den, Inc.
3417 Rochester Road
Royal Oak, MI 48073

Mohave Industries, Inc.
2365 Northern Ave.
Kingman, AZ 86401

Moon's Rock Shop
601 Orchard Drive
Twin Falls, ID 83301

The Naja
10671 Melody Drive
Northglenn, CO 80234

Nelson The Rocky-Feller, Inc.
1509 West 6th Avenue
Eugene, OR 97402

99 Rock Shop
1185 Chambers
Eugene, OR 97402

Novell's Craft Supply
Suite 106-1011 Colesville Rd.
Silver Springs, MD 20901

Nutmeg Minerals
Haddam Quarter Road
Durham, CN 06422

Oklahoma Lapidary Supply
Route 6, Box 9-1
Ponca City, OK 74601

Pathfinder Minerals
41942 Via San Gabriel
Fremont, CA 94538

Patrick's Rock Shop
9101 Malvern Drive
Parma, OH 44129

Pearson's Stone Craft
5128 Auburn Blvd.
P.O. Box 41672
Sacramento, CA 95841

The Pebble Pups, Inc.
Box 2677
Mesilla, NM 88046

Peck's Rock Shop
682 West Division St.
Nipomo, CA 93444

Peck's Rock Shop
4605 W. Columbia Ave.
Battle Creek, MI 49017

The Pioneer
4516 Dixie Highway
Drayton Plains, MI 48020

Poppy Jasper Rock Shop
P.O. Box 127
34 Muckelemi Street
San Juan Bautista, CA 95045

The Pyramid
535 C Street
San Diego, CA 92101

Quality Rock Shop
Route 1, Box 211
Canyon, TX 79015

S. C. Ralys
265 West River Street
Orange, MA 01364

Red & Green Minerals
415 West 24
Hutchinson, KS 67501

Redondo Gems & Mineral
Company
1426 Aviation Blvd.
Redondo Beach, CA 90278

Repeat Rock Shop
400 Lincoln Way
Auburn, CA 95603

The Ringmaker Store
314 Mitchell Street
Turlock, CA 95380

Rio Grande Jewelers Supply,
Inc.
6901 Washington Northeast
Albuquerque, NM 87109

The Rock & Shell Shop
6070 Southwest 8th Street
Miami, FL 33144

The Rock Shop
P.O. Box 611, U.S. 98 East
Gulf Breeze, FL 32561

Rocks, Rings & Other Things
71 Military Road
Buffalo, NY 14027

Rocks To Riches, Inc.
213 West Dundee Road
Buffalo Grove, IL 60090

Rojan Rock 'N Hobby Center
255 Michigan Street
Bandon, OR 97411

Ron & Fran's Rock Shop
Route 1, Box 43
Daytona Beach, FL 32014

Ron's Rocks & Fine Gifts
3037 Tremainsville
Toledo, OH 43613

Russ' Gem & Minerals
1419 West Elm Street
Lodi, CA 95240

Rutlader Company
Wornall Plaza Center
8247 Wornall Road
Kansas City, MO 64114

Salem Gem & Craft Shop
West Clemonsville Road
(Carsinal Shopping Center)
Winston-Salem, NC 27107

San Juan Gems
P. O. Box 1077
(North Dolores Highway)
Cortez, CO 81321

Santa Anita Rocks & Minerals
113 East Huntington Drive
Arcadia, CA 91006

Science Hobbies, Inc.
2615 Central Ave.
Charlotte, NC 28205

Seabrook
135 Third Street
San Rafael, CA 94901

Sempert's
6719 East Napier
Benton Harbor, MI 49022

The 1776 Shop
5559 East Virginia Blvd.
Norfolk, VA 23502

Shamrock Rock Shop
593 West La Cadena Drive
Riverside, CA 92501

Shiela's Rock Shop
10412-118 Avenue
Edmonton, Alberta,
Canada T5G   0P7

Norman J. Shoemaker
Company
541 South Drexel Ave.
Columbus, OH 43209

The Silver Cache
6440 South McClintock
Tempe, AZ 85283

The Silver Dream
711 Greenwood
Jackson, MI 49204

Silver Fox Trading Post
1402 Las Vegas Blvd.
Las Vegas, NV 89104

Silvercraft
7105 University Ave.
La Mesa, CA 92041

Silversmith
6136 Highway 290 West
Austin, TX 78735

The Silversmith, Inc.
3025 South Main
Las Cruses, NM 88001

Silver's Stone Age
Route 31
Pemington, NJ 08534

Skipper's III Inc. Rock Shop
2409 North Cocoa Blvd.
Cocoa, FL 32922

Smokey Mountain Rock Shop
Box 6050
Fort Myers Beach, FL 33931

Southwestern Minerals
7008 Central Ave. Southeast
Albuquerque, NM 87108

Spragg's Rocks & Gems
1501 West 13th Street
Davenport, IA 52804

Stan's Shop
123 West 500 North
Provo, UT 84601

Starlite Gems & Minerals
4131 East Van Buren
Phoenix, AZ 85008

Starlite Rock & Gem Shop
805 Century Drive
Dubuque, IA 52001

Sternwest, Division of
   Sterndent
2330 Beverly Blvd.
Los Angeles, CA 90057

Stonecraft, Inc.
27 South High Street
Dublin, OH 43017

Stoney's Rocks
10702 Apache Trail
P.O. Box 1098
Apache Junction, AZ 85220

Terry's Lapidary
3616 East Gage Ave.
Bell, CA 90201

Tervo's House of Specialties
14 Nassau Blvd. South
Garden City, NY 11530

Texas Mineral Supply
2508 North Ayers Ave.
Fort Worth, TX 76103

Thomas' Rock Hobby Supplies
3141 Fairview Street
Davenport, IA 52804

Treasure of the Pirates
4840 Rugby Ave.
Bethesda, MD 20014

Tucker's Lapidary Hawaii
693-A Mapunapuna Street
Honolulu, HI 96819

Tyler Mountain Lapidary
5257 Big Tyler Road
Charleston, WV 25312

V-Rock Shop
6992 Chippewa Northeast
North Canon, OH 44720

Vacationland Rocks
107 Center Street
Sanford, MI 48657

Valley Rock Shop
9319 East Trent Ave.
Spokane, WA 99206

Walters Lapidary
10250–82 Street
Edmonton, Alberta,
Canada T6A   3M3

Wash-Dak-Cal Gunsmith &
Gem Shop
22745 Ramona Ave.
Apple Valley, CA 92307

Western Gem & Mineral Supplies
Box 219, Aldergrove
British Columbia, Canada
V0X   1A0

Western Montana Gem & Lapidary Supply
No. 2 Lewis and Clark Drive
Lolo, MT 59847

Worldwide Gems & Minerals, Inc.
2604 21st Street
Sacramento, CA 95818

Zymex
900 West Los Vallecitos Blvd.
San Marcos, CA 92069

INDEX